Lead the
Pack

Sparking innovation that
drives customers wild

Lead the
Pack

Sparking innovation that drives customers wild

Nelson Soken, Ph.D.
Wil Wengert

Mill City Press, Inc.
212 3rd Avenue North, Suite 570
Minneapolis, MN 55401
612.455.2294
www.millcitypublishing.com

ISBN - 978-1-934937-45-7
ISBN - 1-934937-45-2
LCCN - 2008940299

Cover Design by Brent Meyers
Typeset by Tiffany Laschinger

Printed in the United States of America

Acknowledgments

To Leslie, Emmaline, and Evan. You are the best cheer-leaders anyone could have. In particular, I acknowledge the contributions of my wife, Leslie, who has always believed in me and supported me with steadfast love. She read every word of the book and provided critical feedback at every point of the project. I also acknowledge the constant support of my mother, my late father, and the whole Soken clan, a sister and four brothers, in Hawaii. You gave me the lessons and love that got me to where I am today. Finally, I would like to thank Beth Bullemer for creating the original graphics and the Mill City Press staff for their assistance and support in the publication process.

~Nelson Soken

To my mother Elizabeth and her late father, Wally, who always supported me in a positive way and never stopped believing in the paths I chose, however unconventional. To Spencer, who offers unconditional love in an age when society rarely rewards or recognizes its true value. To my son Houston and my daughter Keerstyn, for their ability to see through the pretense and feel the genetic strength of a family bond that endures both time and distance. Finally, to my friend and colleague Nelson Soken, when presented with the raw theory of complementary innovation, he provided the majority of the time and contribution in building the framework that supports its overall application with creativity and dedication I never thought possible. Thank you all!

~Wil Wengert

Contents

Foreword

In my twenty years as an R&D executive at 3M, Imation, and Honeywell, I continually struggled to balance the requests of innovators for more money, resources, and time, on one hand, and the demands of the corporation for less investment, more speed, and better results.

Year after year 3M inducts into their Carlton Society individuals who have made significant contributions to 3M's commercial success. The members are an elite group of the most revered innovators and/or contributors at 3M. When speaking to these inductees one-on-one, I discovered that their success was based on their persistence and ability to overcome organizational and management resistance to their ideas. Our best innovators had succeeded in spite of the organization (which, by the way, was quite supportive of innovation).

Soken and Wengert offer a new lens through which to view this conundrum. They focus on the human side of innovation. They provide an in-depth explanation of how an understanding of human nature and psychology can unlock the power of creativity in organizations and employees, and increase customer acceptance of new ideas. Why do people, whether customers or organizations or individual employees, think and behave the way they do? Soken and Wengert take the reader on an innovation journey, from uncovering innovations with customer value to molding the innovation into a concept that can be validated with customers and assessed by the company for development feasibility, and to nurturing and shepherding the innovation to fruition.

Soken and Wengert also provide practical advice and tips on improving innovation efforts from the perspective of the customer and the organization. Successful innovation requires an understanding and deep appreciation of the psychology of customers and organizations. How to uncover what customers' need or desire before they even know it? How to get customer feedback early and often? How to build customer excitement and demand? On the flip side, how to get internal company support and, more importantly, reduce active resistance? How to build a culture of innovation that is continually creating innovations and reinventing itself? These are the types of issues that Soken and Wengert address in this book.

This is an important book that can unblock your organization and lead to greater business success and professional satisfaction.

Krzysztof K. Burhardt Ph.D.

Chairman of the Board Analysts International Corp, partner at Clotho and Associates, former VP of R&D 3M, CTO of Imation, and VP of Technology at Honeywell Inc.

Introduction

The Innovation Journey:
Mastering the mental mysteries of the human mind

> *"This 'telephone' has too many shortcomings to be seriously considered as a means of communication. The device is inherently of no value to us."*
>
> ~Western Union memo response regarding the telephone in 1876.

> *"The horse is here to stay, the automobile is only a fad."*
>
> ~president of Michigan Savings Bank to Horace Rackham, lawyer for Henry Ford in 1903.

Winning and losing in today's marketplace happens at break-neck speed. Companies have to continually innovate to serve customers and stay ahead of the competition. Companies that do not keep pace risk becoming extinct. "Innovative firms--those which are able to use innovation to differentiate their products and services from competition--are on average twice as profitable as other firms."[1]

When you think of innovative companies, which ones come to mind? Apple? Google? 3M? Toyota? Microsoft? GE? These are the ones most often mentioned in the business press, but there are plenty of others. What are these companies doing that others aren't? Is it their monetary investment? Apple CEO Steve Jobs doesn't think so. "Innovation has nothing to do with how many R&D dollars you have. When Apple came up with the Mac, IBM was spending at least one hundred times more on R&D. It's not about money. It's about the people you have, how you're led, and how much you get it."[2] Jobs' observation is confirmed by research. There is no correlation between R&D spending and corporate success as measured in growth and profitability. The only exception is that too little spending definitely has a negative effect.[3] Despite whatever money and time is invested, customers end up rejecting 80-90 percent of new products and services.[4,5,6]

This profoundly high failure rate for innovation begs at least two questions:

1. Why do consumers reject so many new products and services?

2. Why, despite all of the R&D money invested in the latest technology, market research, and business acumen available, can't companies improve their success rate for new products?

What does it take to survive and thrive in today's marketplace? What secret sauce or magic do some companies have that other companies don't? The answer lies in an understanding of human psychology, and the ability to leverage this knowledge within your company and with customers. Innovation is a product of the human imagination and creativity. Leaders need to deliberately act with the knowledge of the underlying psychological mechanisms of WHY people behave the way they do, which helps them determine HOW to proceed and WHAT to do to fix the issues.

Successful innovators are able to manage innovation from the people side. By understanding the forces that shape thinking and influence behavior, they are able to truly identify customer needs, even when customers don't know or can't articulate what those needs really are. At the same time, these innovators are able to deal with the organizational issues that hinder innovation.[7] They are able to create a safe and nurturing environment that encourages taking intelligent risks, collaboration across organizational boundaries, and to truly seek deep customer insights. Just as importantly, these leaders of innovation recognize that it takes time and investment to rewire their organizational DNA to one that fully embraces innovation.

The book is organized as follows:

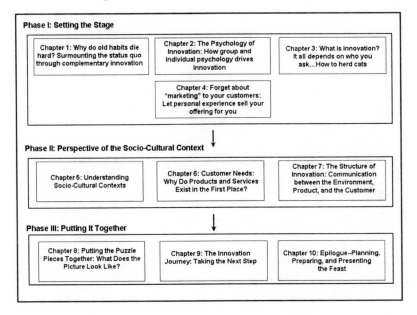

Figure I.1

Those who understand and effectively manage the psychological dynamics occurring in the midst of innovation activities have significant competitive advantage. Leaders need to understand how psychological factors affect how people respond to new ideas and solutions and how they deal with uncertainty. This book will equip you to develop an innovation mindset that can be applied in a variety of situations.

Drawing on the fields of cognitive psychology, business strategy, human factors/user-centered design/usability, marketing, and innovation research, a map is drawn that serves as a guidance system that can be used to prevent travel down many dead-end paths. Each chapter provides theoretical background, illustrative examples, and specific tips and questions to encourage you to explicitly think about how personal biases, experiences, and knowledge gaps either support or discourage innovation. Armed with these valuable insights, leaders will be prepared to address the ever-increasing expectations for more and faster innovations in the marketplace. Let's spark innovation as we begin our innovation journey together.

"We treat innovation as if it were magical, not subject to guidance or nurturing, much less planning. If we study history, however, we know that's simply not true."

~S.J. Palmisano (2003)[8]

Chapter 1

. . . .

Why do old habits die hard? Surmounting the status quo through complementary innovation

"Change is hard because people overestimate the value of what they have—and underestimate the value of what they may gain by giving that up."

~James Belasco and Ralph Stayer

"You will either step forward into growth or you will step back into safety."

~Abraham Maslow

Step back in time and into the shoes of the early creators of some technologies we now take for granted: airplanes, telephones and automobiles. In their early stages, newfangled ideas were scorned more than praised. What if the creators of these technologies listened to the doubts of potential customers, trusted advisors, the general public and, sometimes, themselves? In 1901, a famous visionary declared, "Man will not fly for fifty years." That was Wilbur Wright and, two years later, his brother Orville made history with the first manned flight at Kitty Hawk. How was the automobile viewed in the early days? The spokesman for Daimler Benz said, "There will never be a mass market for motor cars—about a thousand in Europe—because that is the limit on the number of chauffeurs available!"

The path from idea to action is a rocky one. Why is it that most people responsible for what we think of as innovation – designers, engineers, scientists, inventors, R&D managers, upper executives, etc. – spend most of their time failing at the very activity upon which their success depends?

The Status Quo: Resistance to Change

Resistance to change and an aversion to taking risks are opposing or retarding forces against innovation. The following passage from Bruce Wilkinson's book, *The Dream Giver*, captures the challenge innovators face when trying to change engrained customer habits and routines:[1]

"For the most part, not much happened in Familiar that hadn't happened before. Ordinary thought he was content. He found the routines reliable. He blended in with the crowd. And mostly, he wanted only what he had. Until the day Ordinary noticed a small, nagging feeling that something big was missing from his life. Or maybe the feeling was that he was missing something big."

What motivates the world's Ordinarys to change or to instill in them that nagging feeling that they are missing something big? Innovations, even the best ones, push people outside of their comfort zone. People generally respond to change in naturally defensive ways either with active resistance or with complacency, because they are attached to the status quo. Innovators need a deep understanding of the contextual dynamics preserving the customer's current routine and keeping things in stasis, as well as a large enough vision to see how these dynamics can be altered or improved. People generally do not change unless their level of dissatisfaction is great and the risk of change is so low because the alternative has clearly demonstrated benefits that people have already realized. In some cases, change is forced upon people whether they want it or not. Even when change is imposed upon people, resistance is reduced when there are clear benefits.

Why do people find change so difficult and where does the resistance come from? Psychological and sociological factors influence people's reaction to innovation but, generally speaking, people resist change and defend the status quo to maintain equilibrium and stability and avoid chaos and disruption, especially when the status quo has been good to them. Innovation always initiates change, the consequences of change are usually uncertain, and uncertainty breeds fear. This fear of change creates barriers to the acceptance and adoption of innovation.

What makes change difficult? Psychologist John Bowlby's (1969) developmental pathway theory provides an appropriate and easy-to-understand metaphor for describing why change is so difficult over time.[2] Bowlby theorized that as we go through life and make "choices," or are pushed in particular directions, we all end up taking different paths. The metaphor he used was the growth of a tree.

A tree starts out with a trunk. Over time, as the limbs and branches grow and diverge, they are farther and farther apart from the trunk. The limbs and branches that grow away from the trunk of the tree are similar to people's experiences on different paths. For example, if a person's experience takes him or her down path A, and circumstances force the person to make a change, it would be easier to shift to path B versus Paths C or D because of the distance he or she must traverse. Furthermore, change in general becomes more difficult over time because of the shift in direction that is required and the increased distance that needs to be traversed. Eventually, the branches and limbs grow outward and apart from the trunk, becoming stronger, harder, thicker, and less flexible.

By analogy, this natural process of growth in human experi-

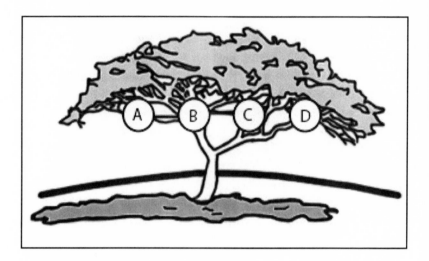

Figure 1.1

ence creates the status quo and a seeming inability to change. As we age, change is harder and harder to embrace, especially radical, disruptive change because of the effort it takes to change in a significant way (e.g., distance to traverse). Most people have established ingrained habits and routines. Change is accepted reluctantly and people prefer not to be disrupted or surprised with new circumstances. How often do we cling to certain ways of doing things and continue to use the same products and services (e.g., cereal, toothpaste)?

Surmounting the Status Quo through Complementary Innovation

By understanding the psychology of human behavior, it is possible to create innovative offerings that customers go wild for and that differentiate you from the competition. We call this type of innovation **complementary innovation**. The term complementary is defined as "to make complete or perfect" or, perhaps, bringing together things in a way that creates value that adds up to more than the sum of its parts. **Complemen-**

tary innovation focuses on the design of a superior customer experience between customers and the offering. The design also takes into account the socio-cultural context in which the experience takes place. Peter Mayle, author of *French Lessons*, captured the essence of a **complementary innovation** experience when he described a dining experience in France: "It wasn't only because of what I had eaten, although that had been incomparably better than anything I'd eaten before. It was the total experience: the elegance of the table setting, the ritual of opening and tasting the wine, the unobtrusive efficiency of the waiters and their attention to detail, arranging the plates just so, whisking up bread crumbs from the tablecloth. For me, it had been a special occasion." (1991).[3]

Complementary innovation assesses a broad set of factors that affect whether customers will change or not. People's willingness to change requires them to be sufficiently dissatisfied with the current solutions, be supported and encouraged to change, and have a sufficient vision of what the change will be like. Getting a vision of what an alternative solution is clearer with direct experience. Deciding where to push, when, and how hard, is critical. Determining how much change customers can bear can be a gauge of whether innovations will be accepted and adopted. Figure out what is not working now, look at what is available and only develop what is missing. The goal is to introduce change in a way that minimizes resistance to acceptance. Excitement is created by providing customers with what they could not even envision was possible.

Timing of Change in the Innovation Life Cycle

Anyone introducing an innovation is challenged to understand what phase in the innovation life cycle current solutions will be found. Everett Rogers's diffusion theory describes how new ideas, such as products and services, are adopted over time.[4] Diffusion is a social communication phenomenon that occurs when a new idea spreads from one person to the next in a consistent, predictable pattern that resembles an S-shaped curve.

The S-curve represents the cumulative number of adopters over time (see Figure 1.2). Early in the diffusion process, few individuals are willing to accept and adopt a new idea. Gradually, the rate of adoption accelerates until all, or almost all, individuals of a social group have adopted the new idea or innovation, which represents the end of the adoption cycle of that particular idea.

Over time, three specific phases of the innovation life cycle should be assessed: the initial phase, when the S-curve has matured, and the transition to a new S-curve. In all three cases, customers' experiences are compared, and the comparison serves as a foundation for how the new complementary offering will be designed.

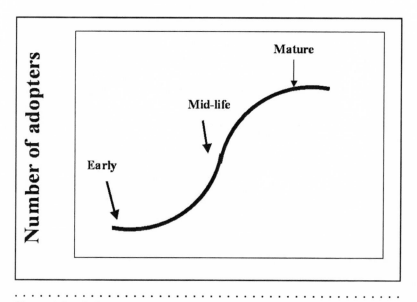

Figure 1.2 – S-Curve

Conquering the initial hump

After a new idea has turned into a real offering, the first challenge is to attract people to the idea. In his 1995 book, *Inside the Tornado*, G.A. Moore theorizes that a chasm exists between the first two adoption groups (innovators/technology enthusiasts and early adopters/visionaries) and the three later adopter categories (early majority/pragmatists, late majority/conservatives, and laggards/skeptics).[5] This chasm exists because, once the initial groups of adopters have bought into the idea, the challenge is to encourage enough people to jump on the bandwagon of a new idea or product to pull it through the middle of the idea's life cycle, where momentum carries the adoption to maturity (see Figure 1.3). The goal is to create a contagious, almost infectious, desire for the offering, by reducing resistance and creating attraction or resonance toward the offering because it meets each individual's unique needs so that they are willing to take risks and abandon the status quo. So-called "must-have" offerings generate enough cultural energy or pent up demand to reach the point where a critical mass of customers clamors to adopt the change rather than resist it.

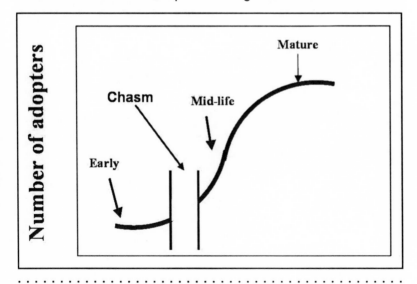

Figure 1.3–Chasm with an S-Curve

Layering and Enriching New Experiences on an Existing Maturing S-Curve

The second challenge, while the idea matures, is to differentiate the offering and maintain profit margins, which becomes difficult with increased competition. This leads to a saturated market where there is fierce, cutthroat competition for established customers, which Kim and Mauborgne (2005) refer to as a red (bloody) ocean.[6] So, how do companies build on past successes and gently challenge the status quo for established customers while also attracting new customers? We call this layering and enriching, whereby the company creates a new experience on an existing base (see Figure 1.4). The goal is to identify and create new experiences that tap the sweet spot between unchanging and changing, old and new, stasis and revolution, and attract customers who will perceive the offering as new. This approach is a two-for-one deal. Attract "early adopters" of the enriched approach who are actually new customers, while at the same time energizing and exciting established customers with the new experience.

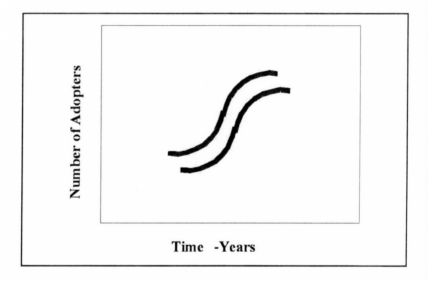

Figure 1.4– Layering and Enriching S-Curve

Transitioning to the Next S-Curve

A third challenge to be resolved is how to reduce disruption and disequilibrium in the transition between S-curves to attract various types of people to the new idea as quickly as possible. Leverage enough of the current S-curve so that customers can anchor themselves in familiarity while at the same time creating a solution that customers perceive as new, exciting, and superior. Is it possible to push the new S-curve close enough to the current S-curve so that the gap is reduced and a bridge is available to cross? Yes. We call this third challenge "crossing the deep, dark, and echoing abyss," because of the difficulty in layering the customer experience in multiple, overlapping S-curves that can bridge the chasm (see Figure 1.5).

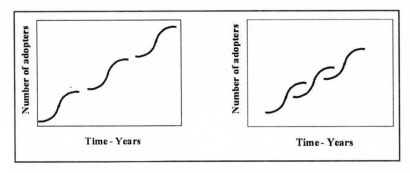

Figure 1.5–Abyss between S-Curves

An innovation mindset takes into account the psychological mechanisms that create resistance to change and the desire to preserve the status quo, as well as to proactively use the psychological knowledge to design customer experiences that actually generate customer energy to pursue and accept/ adopt innovation. For example, in a mature market, a company should recognize the psychological barriers and avoid fighting it out with competitors for current customers. Instead, pursue new customers who are not bound by the status quo. Design a customer experience that leverages current company capabilities while customizing it for those new customers. Simultaneously, identify other companies that might resist and be actively hostile to its entry. Find ways of creating complementary relationships wherein everyone benefits.[7] By looking at the psychology of resistance, and pursuing a *complementary innovation strategy*, companies increase the likelihood of success and the adoption of their innovative offering.

Manager Key Takeaways

Fighting the status quo requires battling the inertia created by time and experience. The battle is fierce because the status quo infects and infiltrates the hearts and minds of the individuals who reside in companies as well as their customers. Individuals in companies who have been successful under the current organizational order will defend the status quo to protect their interests and maintain their level of comfort. Customers resist change because they are comfortable with the current way of doing things. Managers need to take a step back and create an environment that encourages the generation of new and original ideas. Brainstorming and creativity activities are only successful if people are encouraged to go beyond the current state of affairs. There are many books on creativity, and the point of all of them is to exercise the mind to avoid falling into a rut: reverse, subtract, add, multiply, eliminate, force random connections, use analogies and metaphors, do more of, or start doing, do less of, or stop doing, combining, do differently, and throw out assumptions. Stop making excuses, start exercising your mind, and don't quit! Always, deliberately do mental calisthenics to continue to stretch your mind so that you don't fall into complacency and become part of the status quo. Five perspectives to take when fighting the status quo:

- **Leverage the Beginner's Mind:** The Power of Naiveté: Force yourself to consider the possibilities from the perspective of someone who is not wedded to the current order of things. Engage people with beginner's minds who can view the world without all of the baggage and ask, "Why can't we do it differently?"

- **Mix it Up:** Use the power of diversity of thought when creating teams to solve problems. Gerard Kleisterlee, CEO of Philips Electronics, noted in a 2004 industry speech: "Overall, I think we need to employ more anthropologists and fewer technologists."[8] When developing a new product, companies too often focus on technological performance, functionality, and manufacturing constraints, without paying enough attention to how the product will actually perform in the customer's hands. Jim Wicks, chief designer for Motorola, has a design staff that goes far beyond typical engineering, including sociologists, psychologists, musicologists, graphic designers, and color experts. Why? Because he believes a full understanding of the human being interacting with Motorola's products will yield more intelligent, user-friendly product designs.[9] Regardless of the industry or the nature of your offering (whether product, service, or technical in nature), mix it up and create diverse groups of smart people who are able to think beyond the status quo.

- **Be a Stranger in a Strange Land:** View the world outside of the current context and current reality like an alien might: Find out how other smart people have solved a similar problem elsewhere. If you focus on your competitors and only talk about the issues with yourself, chances are you will come up with incremental improvements and solutions. By seeking inspiration from outside of the current context, it is possible to identify potential solutions that you would not have thought of. Look to nature. Look to other cultures. Look to other industries. Look to new people in the organization. Look to people who could be new customers.

- **Empty the Old Box Before you Think Outside of it:** Foster an environment of patience and diligence so that people generate a truly diverse set of ideas from brainstorming activities. This requires using methods to solicit ideas from different types of people (e.g., introverts/extroverts, varied experience and expertise, etc.) and to discourage people from jumping on the first good idea. The initial ideas generated tend to be incremental and less creative because they are usually based on the status quo and current assumptions. New ideas are generated after all the old ideas are emptied from people's minds and there is time to create new connections. Give people the opportunity to bounce ideas off of each other so that the ideas can be built upon.

- **What If and Why Not?** Test assumptions and preconceived expectations: Implicit and explicit assumptions greatly influence the status quo. Over time, we view the world through a filter of assumptions and expectations. The challenge is to explicitly question those expectations and assumptions, and then manipulate them to create new potential futures and scenarios. Encourage people to make their assumptions explicit to create a shared understanding. Then, manipulate the assumptions to see how the world could be. Ask yourself: What would be possible if new assumptions were put in place or if old assumptions were changed or thrown out?

Keep in mind these fresh perspectives so you can avoid being entangled in the status quo even as you read this book. Niccolo Machiavelli said: "...there is nothing more difficult to take in hand, more perilous to conduct, or more uncertain in its success, than to take the lead in the introduction of a new order of things. Because the innovator has for enemies all those who have done well under the old conditions, and lukewarm defenders in those who may do well under the new." However, if you don't take on the challenge of fighting against the old order of things and innovating, you risk failure. Sir Francis Bacon warned, "He that will not apply new remedies can expect new evils, for time is the greatest innovator."

Chapter 2

The Psychology of Innovation: How group and individual psychology drives innovation

"Nothing is more dangerous than a dogmatic worldview-nothing more constraining, more blinding to innovation, more destructive of openness to novelty"

--Stephen Jay Gould

Organizational groups are not unlike the boys in William Golding's classic novel *Lord of the Flies*, in which different groups develop their own rituals, language, and views of the company while competing for limited resources for survival. Marketing professionals see innovation from a marketing perspective. People from R&D see it from an R&D perspective. Manufacturing sees it from a manufacturing perspective. Technologists see it from a technology perspective, and so on. In many cases, each functional area thinks they understand the issues clearly, and that those in the other areas are more likely to be clueless. This simple but pervasive challenge in organizations results in a lack of communication and coordination between departments, which leads to misunderstanding.

Many books have been written that describe the inner workings of innovative companies. With all these resources available, why is it that companies can't instantly transform themselves into successful innovators? The reason companies are unable to easily imitate success is that innovation is not about a secret recipe or process; it is about culture and human psychology. Creating innovations begins with a deeper awareness of why people are the way they are, why they make the decisions they do, and why people's actions aren't always rational, even when they may seem so on the surface. Let's begin to unravel the underlying psychological mechanisms that create resistance to innovation and, if dealt with appropriately, motivate people to innovate and to accept change.

Cultural Influences: The Power of Many

As Renaissance poet John Donne wrote: "No man is an island, entire of itself; every man is a piece of the continent." A simple way of thinking about the importance of cultural context is to recognize that customers care about what others think of them. According to Charles Horton Cooley, people define themselves by how they believe other people see them (theory known as the "looking-glass self"). Culture provides social constraints (blueprints for individual behavior within a culture) that influence how we assimilate and respond to our environment. Innovations must fit within the cultural context, be perceived as reflecting and reinforcing cultural values and norms, and generate positive *cultural energy* that encourages acceptance and adoption of the innovation. Everyone realizes that the broader culture influences people's behavior. But how do we take this into account when identifying opportunities, designing solutions, and launching into the marketplace? For example, if individualism, achievement, success, and material comfort are core values, product and services such as luxury cars and high-end real estate will be positively perceived as evidence of success.

A model developed by Urie Bronfenbrenner (1979) provides guidance on how to make sense of the broader cultural context and how various psychological and cultural factors influence the customer[1] (Further described in Chapter 5). By appreciating these factors it is possible to anticipate how an offering will fit into the context, and make appropriate design and marketing decisions.

Bronfenbrenner's model is represented below:

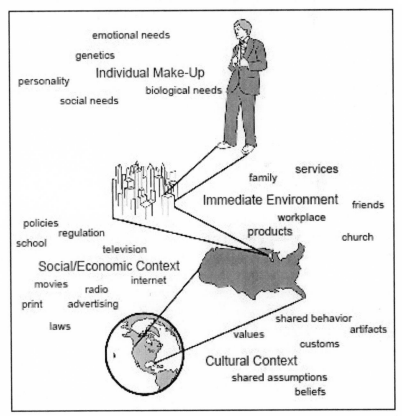

Figure 2.1

With this as a backdrop innovation leaders/managers need to consider the following:

Cultural values and norms

The vast majority, if not everyone in a company, has experienced values and norms initiatives designed to strengthen company morale and alignment. If you suspend your cynicism and the "Dilbert filter," values and norms have a powerful influence on people's views toward innovation. Cultural values define ideas about what a desirable life is, what is good and bad, beautiful and ugly, acceptable and unacceptable. Norms develop out of a group's values and describe the rules of behavior and expectations of the group. When people either follow or break the norms, there are positive or negative sanctions. Thus, values and norms influence people's view of what is worthwhile and preferred, providing a guide for behavioral choices and "rules of the road." For example, Google created a culture of "creative fearlessness and ambition." Salter describes Google's culture: "When you visit the Googleplex in Mountain View, California, what makes it special is elusive. The company looks like the standard-issue, Wii-in-the-lounge, hieroglyphs-on-a-whiteboard, code-until-dawn tech shop. The difference isn't tangible. It's in the air, in the spirit of the place. In the end, the resources and liberty that Google entrusts to its workers infuses them with a rare sense of possibility—and obligation."[2]

Shifts in social values and norms regarding personal health has led to an increase in society's comfort level with personal medical topics. Television commercials during primetime now openly refer to prostate health, erectile dysfunction, and menopause. Such emerging shifts in cultural values and norms directly influence the discovery of opportunities. Case in point: Viagra. Dr. Alan Hillman observed, "I don't think our society would have accepted the marketing or selling of a drug for erectile dysfunction as recently as 20-25 years ago...The drug discovery process is now and always has been an 'aha' experience." David Brinkley of Pfizer suggested that "Maybe 10-20 years ago, if we had seen the exact same effect [male erection as side effect of medication for angina and blood pressure] we would have dismissed it and said, 'Oh, it's all in their heads.'" The point is that the innovation process, particularly the discovery and marketing introduction phases, are influenced by social values and norms concerning what is and is not acceptable. As Dr. Hillman asserted, "You need the right researcher at the right moment in history."[3]

Subcultures

One way of looking at segmentation is to identify subcultures and countercultures. Subcultures share values and norms that are compatible with the dominant culture although they have a distinctive way of looking at life. Countercultures, on the other hand, have values and norms that are in direct opposition to the dominant culture. What social standings are the subcultures trying to achieve, and what status symbols do they use to identify themselves? Understanding how these subcultures or counterculture groups fit into the general society provides a unique perspective on innovation. Consider Harley-Davidson motorcycle riders, or extreme adventure sports enthusiasts, or the rapper subculture. These groups may come from different walks of life, but they share passions that, when harnessed, can generate significant company growth. When positioned correctly, offerings that originally started out in subcultures spill into the general culture and become mainstream offerings.

An emerging subculture that draws fans from the sought after 18-34 year-old-male demographic (and an increasing number of women) is mixed martial arts tournaments that include the UFC (Ultimate Fighting Championship) and IFL (International Fight League). The once "no holds barred" fighting contests that were once compared to human cockfighting have emerged as a legitimate sporting event. The UFC is on Spike TV as well as pay-per-view with matches being held in Las Vegas. One match brought in twenty million dollars in pay-per-view and ticket sales. The IFL will be broadcast on Fox and their sponsors include Sandals Resorts, Xbox, Suzuki, and

Mickey's beer.[4] Clearly, there is a subculture (for some it could be considered a counterculture) willing to pay to see modern gladiators fight each other until they are often bloody and/or knocked senseless.

Conformity: Following the majority

Conformity to group pressure plays a major role in the acceptance and adoption of innovation. A desire to be a part of a group and not perceived as different creates a great deal of resistance to change. A famous experiment on group behavior and conformity showed that individuals can be influenced by the group, even when the group was clearly responding incorrectly.[5] Individuals were asked to select the line in Exhibit 2 that matches the length of the line in Exhibit 1.

Obviously, the answer is that line A in Exhibit 2 is the same length as the line in Exhibit 1. However, people in the group working for the experimenter selected an incorrect response.

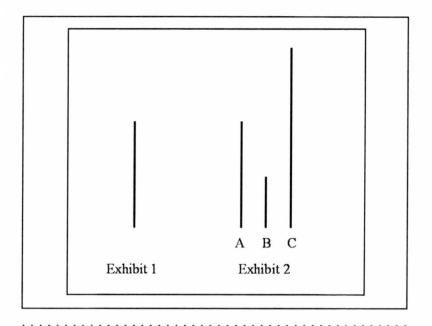

Figure 2.2

Test participants went along with the incorrect choice 37 percent of the time – even though the correct answer was obvious! Innovation is breaking away from established ways of looking at the world, in essence, being nonconformist. If, in a controlled experiment, individuals can be influenced by strangers 37 percent of the time to choose the wrong answer even if the correct answer is obvious, we clearly must first understand why people tend to conform to majority opinion if we are to innovate. Reasons for conformity include:[6]

- People will go along with the group because they believe the group is right and/or that the group has information they don't and, therefore, knows better.

- People sometimes conform, even if they disagree, to avoid embarrassment and/or make an impression on people whom they would like to associate with or emulate. Sometimes it is an attempt to achieve a certain social status.

- People sometimes conform because they are told to do so by authority figures or the group in power, in which case people abdicate responsibility to the authority. Sometimes consumers appear to be gullible drones because they seem to "just do what they are told" if the expert in the white coat claims that the product will help them, for example, to lose weight in one week.

Conformity to the cultural values and norms of a group, and the desire to fit in within the group, are powerful psychological forces to use in influencing people toward innovation. For example, Flores, Letelier, and Spinosa (2003) found that successful attitude and behavior change in emerging markets was achieved when existing cultural practices and social networks were incorporated into business practices.[7] In essence, people can be encouraged to accept and adopt innovation by creating support systems compatible with existing social systems which leverages their tendency to conform to group values and norms to fit in. Techniques to strengthen the social glue and increase individual trust and loyalty included (a) using already existing social practices such as informal community savings clubs promotes a sense of meaning and familiarity. This makes change more comfortable and safe, (b) creating support groups that help people achieve their goals faster while at the same time providing emotional support in the process to make it feel less risky and scary; (c) using local community leaders as spokespersons to spread the message via word of mouth, increasing the level of credibility and trust in the product/service, and (d) using people who have already been successful as advocates and promoters for the product/service.

Individual Influences: How the Mind Filters

As we all know, understanding individual human behavior is not an easy task. However, human beings share some common ways of thinking that influence how the acceptance and adoption process unfolds.

Overcoming Egocentrism: People see the world through individual lenses.

All the experiences that people have form the expectations and assumptions that guide the way they think, act, and interpret events in the world. These mental structures are known as schemas. Based on these experiences, people develop lenses or filters that color how they see everything. Unfortunately this means they judge everything from their own perspective. Jean Piaget (1970), a child psychologist, described a phenomenon in the preschool years called egocentrism that we can often see also in adults.[8] Egocentrism is the tendency to judge everything from one's own perspective because of an inability to see another person's point of view. It's all about my thoughts, my beliefs, my feelings, and my needs and desires. In fact, the tendency to see the world from one's own perspective extends to the point that people will force-fit information into their current belief system or ignore or dismiss information that does not support those beliefs.

Given that people have a tendency to see through their own eyes, an added psychological complexity to deal with is that everyone is different; therefore their experience of the world and what they filter out varies. From birth, people have different temperaments or styles of responding to the world. These characteristics include different levels of activity, adaptability to new situations, intensity, mood, distractibility, and persistence of attention.[9] [10] Furthermore, people also process information differently. Some are visual and want to see pictures; others respond more to numbers and data, while others prefer to hear stories and process information via emotional connectedness and relationships.[11] [12] Natural tendencies, interests, and needs influence what people seek out, are attracted to, what they remember or pay attention to, how they act, what motivates them, and their willingness to try something new and different. Can you see the connection between characteristics attributed to infants, such as "adaptable," "active," "slow to warm up," and familiar descriptions of the willingness of company personnel to take risks and adopt innovations, such as "innovator," "early adopter," and "laggard?"

Egocentrism and personal schemas' relationship to innovation are well represented by Everett Rogers: "An innovation is an idea, practice, or object that is perceived as new by an individual or other unit of adoption. It matters little, so far as human behavior is concerned, whether or not an idea is "objectively" new as measured by the lapse of time since its first use or discovery. The perceived newness of the idea determines the individual's reaction to it. If an idea seems new, it is an innovation."[13] This explains why one person can become so excited about a new toothpaste, new ketchup containers that stand upside down, or colored office supplies, whereas someone else can wonder what the big deal is.

People's tendency to be egocentric means that it is difficult to get everyone on the same page; whether it is people at a company seeing the world in the same way and appreciating each other's differences or getting customers who have diverse views and experiences to adopt an offering because they each see value in it from their unique perspective.

Other psychological principles to keep in mind when it comes to innovation include:

People have an aversion to taking risks, and fear losing what they already have.

The desire to preserve the status quo (and avoid risk) is usually stronger than the desire to upset the status quo, even if a gain on the other end is more likely than not (endowment effect/loss aversion).[14] People also tend to view past events in a more positive light than they actually deserve. For example, once people have adopted a solution and had some experience with it, they tend to forget how much trouble and effort went into the change. In retrospect, the past – no matter how difficult –seems rosy (rosy retrospection), and the future seems fraught with peril. Because of these cognitive biases, anything new is subject to scrutiny, and must prove itself a substantial enough improvement over the old to justify switching.

People tend to think in the concrete here and now, not in the hypothetical future.

Jean Piaget proposed that by adulthood, people are able to think abstractly and hypothetically.[15] Research also suggests that many adults do not often use this cognitive capability. Instead, they function in what Piaget called the "concrete op- erational period," wherein their thinking is tied directly to the physical world.[16]

The implication of this tendency for people to view the world concretely (what is) rather than abstractly (what could be) is that people use the current concrete solution as the reference point for their judgments. Innovation requires people to think in abstract terms because innovation often does not exist or is different to cur- rent offerings. Consequences of a concrete bias are that customers as well as company personnel tend to focus on incremental changes that address their dissatisfaction with the shortcomings of the current solution. Consequently, companies must fight the innate resistance to intangibles and unknowns when pushing innovation given the gap between concrete and abstract thinking. As Steve Jobs concluded, "You can't ask customers what they want and then try to give that to them. By the time you get it built, they'll want something else." People know what they like and don't like about what they currently have, but they have great difficulty imagining what they really want. They will know what they want when they see, touch, and interact with it.

People tend to see only the current use of a solution rather than expanding to new uses.

People tend to view objects as serving only one purpose even if the object can be used for other purposes. Psychologists call this "functional fixedness." Abraham Maslow observed, "If you only have a hammer, you tend to see every problem as a nail."[17] This tendency to be fixated on what something is currently used for or how something currently is experienced has two consequences. First, it limits people's ability to learn from each other. For example, can the way Boeing builds airplanes be compared to McDonalds' making hamburgers or Disney checking in people at rides compared to airline or hotel check-in? The answer is yes, if you see the situation as being similar at some level (e.g., step by step building process and checking people in). Secondly, it limits people's options for fulfilling their needs. This explains why some people keep using the same solution for a particular task even if there are better alternatives. It is fixed in their minds that there is only one way of accomplishing a goal, and the dissatisfaction with the current way has not increased sufficiently to warrant change.

An example of being able to see beyond current applications is the history of a motor originally designed for the Spin Pop lollipop. While scanning the tooth-care aisle of a Wal-Mart, the inventors of the Spin Pop determined that the same motor used for spinning the lollipop could be used to rotate the brushes of an electric toothbrush that ultimately became the Spinbrush (now owned by Procter & Gamble). The same technology was incorporated into another P&G product called the Tide Stainbrush, which is used to remove stains from clothing.

People's processing of the world defies logic.

The information processing theory of human cognition compares thinking to a computer, which logically processes information in steps or in a sequence. But if humans are so logical, why do so many believe they have a higher probability of dying in a plane crash than in an automobile accident, when in fact, statistically speaking they are much more likely to be hurt or killed driving a car? Why is it that gamblers—or, for that matter, investors—believe they are on a hot streak, or that their luck is about to change, even if there is no logical reason for their belief?

Human beings aren't as logical or as rational as we'd like to believe. Emotions and unconscious processing play a much more significant role than previously thought. However, we are also not just a bundle of emotions that drive our behavior. Ultimately, it is a balance of both. Recent brain research using MRI (f-MRI) technology suggests that long-term economic decisions are driven by the part of the brain where rational thought (weighing pros and cons) is centered, whereas short-term decisions, such as whether to buy a chocolate bar, are centered in the part of the brain where emotion is located.[18]

The misguided belief that customers always act rationally can adversely affect how products are created and marketed. Should we focus on convincing customers with a list of features and a handful of facts and logical arguments, or allow the customer to try out the product, experience the benefits, and develop an emotional attachment to the product (e.g., taking home the TV for the big game)?

Better innovation through psychology

Spanish explorer Juan Ponce de Leon supposedly was in search of the Fountain of Youth in 1513 when he traveled to what is now Florida. Unfortunately, not unlike Ponce de Leon, companies are constantly in search of the Fountain of Innovation, whereby a single recipe will deliver a continuous wellspring of innovation. Improving innovation is much more nuanced and requires an awareness of individual and group psychology. Psychology offers important keys to understanding WHY it is so difficult to influence people to change and also provides a deeper appreciation of the human forces at work that encourages and discourages the creation and adoption of innovation. The context of customers and company employees may be different but the same underlying psychological principles of human behavior are operating within both contexts.

An awareness of the underlying psychological mechanisms operating within companies can help those who promote innovation actively manage it. By understanding where resistance to change comes from and why, companies can harness the creative energy needed to innovate effectively. Companies can then better identify, design, evaluate, and market superior customer experiences.

From a customer standpoint, these psychological mechanisms need to be considered when designing the interaction between the customer and the innovation. Successful design is achieved when it seamlessly *communicates* to a customer about how it is supposed to be used, and what its benefits are, and provides such a satisfying experience that it creates enthusiasts who will advocate for the product/service. Below is a representation of the integrated model to innovation based on the work of psychologists James Gibson and Abraham Maslow.[19, 20, 21] The model consists of customer needs on the left side of the graphic, the immediate product/service environment on the right, and the process that governs the interaction between the customer and the product/service. This model will be discussed in greater detail in Chapter 6 and 7.

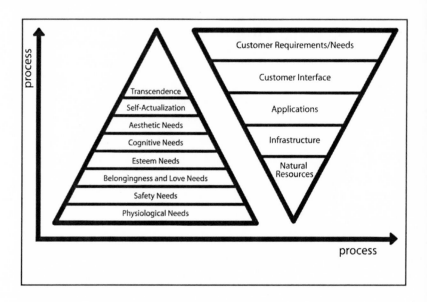

Figure 2.3

Manager Key Takeaways

Turn customers into a free marketing department.

Fighting against the status quo requires leveraging the power of many to create momentum with change.

- Have you identified advocates and allies for change who are willing to push the limits to achieve something new? People are more open to innovation when there is someone else at their side who is voicing opposition to the status quo. Even when people oppose the majority for different reasons, just having someone else in support encourages people to challenge the currently held view. Encourage people who are sitting on the sidelines to perceive less risk to change by having others already on the bandwagon.

- People are more likely to be persuaded to try new things if a credible messenger engages them. Are you using highly credible and influential people in existing social networks as word-of-mouth advocates (viral marketers) to build excitement for the innovation with potential customers?

Leverage customer knowledge to create a segmentation strategy.

Companies need to leverage what they know about how customers think, feel, and behave to fully engage and influence them toward innovation.

- What are you doing to truly appreciate how different types of customers will benefit from your innovation so that you can generate enough interest from enough customers?

- How do you tailor your communication to fit customers' ways of processing information?

- How do you identify customers who have the temperament for trying new things?

- What are you doing to help customers see and experience beyond their current egocentric filters and biases so that they are more likely to change?

- What are you doing to influence customers' minds and hearts (rational, logical, and emotional) toward the innovation rather than assuming only a rational, logical decision-making process?

Give customers concrete experiences with innovations.

"Tell me and I'll forget; show me and I may remember; involve me and I'll understand." (Chinese Proverb): Direct experience forms the basis of a relationship that shapes expectations for future interactions. Direct experience communicates more, in a shorter period of time and more persuasively, than indirect exposure such as talking about a concept. Thus, breaking away from the past requires a concrete and tangible experience of the alternative, especially when the alternative diverges significantly from the current offering. If people don't have a tangible experience to evaluate the differences between the current experience and the alternative they will make assumptions about the alternative. Those assumptions tend to favor the status quo because it is what people are comfortable with. With an experience, people can truly evaluate the alternative rather than depend on flawed assumptions and their imagination, both of which tend to be biased against new things.

- What are you doing to make the benefits of the innovation so apparent to customers that they are willing to give up what they currently have for the innovation?

- Customers can then provide robust feedback and also envision what is possible in the future. Are you taking advantage of all available opportunities to allow customers to directly interact with prototype solutions as early and often as possible?

Chapter 3

**What is innovation?
It all depends on who you ask…
How to herd cats.**

You have been assigned the responsibility by a senior vice president to "accelerate innovation" within your company. You have a free hand to develop the strategy and operational plan. The plan needs to be completed by the next board meeting. What an opportunity!

After the initial excitement and exhilaration, reality sets in. Where do you start? What does the SVP mean by accelerating innovation? How do you come up with a strategy when you don't know what the strategy is for? How do you get all the stakeholders on the same page?

People perceive and think about the world differently, and accommodating these different perspectives is one of the biggest challenges innovators face. The goal of innovation leaders is to align everyone toward a common purpose and to identify and harness everyone's energy toward the same innovation vision. It is the challenge of herding cats.

Piaget (1970) described a concept called *decentering*, which is the transition from being self-centered to considering others' points of view. Successful innovation requires a shared understanding and common perspective on innovation.[1] Different perspectives to keep in mind when managing innovation are:

- Are the benefits of the innovation for customers and/or the company?

- What are people thinking about when they say innovation?

- Is the innovation discussion focused on sustaining the core business and/or disrupting the industry with a new approach or solution?

- Is the paradigm shifting to a new business model?

- Is it process innovation?

- Is it positioning?

- Is it products and services?

Perspective: Innovation Benefits from the Customer or Company Perspective

A subtle but insidious tendency in companies is for leaders to talk as if they are customer-focused when in fact they are actually focused on the company's interests and needs and, to a lesser extent, the customers. Actually, in many cases, leaders have good intentions regarding customers and don't even realize that they are falling into the psychological trap of corporate egocentrism. Managers of innovation must explicitly manage people's perspectives and ensure that the needs of the customer and the company are represented. Consider the various corporate strategies such as Six Sigma, Lean Sigma, and TQM, which are well intentioned but, if not managed correctly, can turn into cost-cutting and corporate process optimization exercises that serve the company at the expense of the customer.

Companies need to take the perspective of the customer as well as their own, and consider customer and company needs on an equal playing field. However, first and foremost, they should always ask themselves: How will any change we make affect the customer experience? Delta Airlines founder C.E. Woolman advised his employees, "Put yourself on the other side of the ticket counter."[2]

A good example of how commonly used concepts can be misinterpreted from a psychological, egocentric perspective is the concepts of disruptive and sustaining innovation or technologies discussed by Clayton Christensen.[3][4] The terms "disruptive" and "sustaining" innovation refers to how companies within an industry respond to core customers, new technologies, and new competitors as a market matures. The core competencies and capabilities of the company and their relationships with other industry players revolve around the current solutions. In particular, it highlights how companies get focused on serving their core customers with sustaining technologies while competitors, both known and unrecognized, are creating disruptive solutions that will unseat the company and transform the industry. The disruption that occurs affects the companies and the industry in terms of how companies operate, relate to each other, and view success. Customers don't want to be disrupted; they just want solutions that improve the quality of their lives. Companies that don't manage the perspective between company and customers can make the mistake of losing their business because they were not truly focusing on the benefits that a wide range of current and potential customers require. Complementary innovation takes into account the customer experience and balances sustaining what customers are familiar with while creating excitement by changing things up just enough (e.g., disruption that creates interest, excitement, and adoption).

Perspective: What do we mean by innovation?

What's the first thing you think of when you hear the word "innovation?" The term "innovation" can mean many things to many people. Is it a fabulous new product, service, or process? It's not unlike John Godfrey Saxe's poem, *The Blind Men and the Elephant*, in which six blind men touch different parts of an elephant and come to different conclusions about the characteristics of an elephant. It's perspective. Everyone is trying to wrap their arms around what innovation is, but they each grab a different part and end up arguing about what the elephant is and what it needs. At the same time, they won't admit that they are blind to the other parts, or recognize that they need each other to truly understand what innovation is all about. Understand that innovation means different things to different people; in essence, innovation is in the *eye of the beholder.*

David Francis and John Bessant, professors in Innovation Management at the Centre for Research in Innovation Management (CENTRIM) in the U.K., devised what they call the "4 Ps of innovation," which describe how innovation takes place:[5]

1. **Paradigm:** Changing the predominant view of the business model of how customers are served and companies execute their business;

2. **Processes:** How things are done;

3. **Positioning:** Who are the customers and how are they communicated to;

4. **Products and services:** What is offered to the customer.

Since innovation can occur in all four areas, companies need to decide where to focus. Generally speaking, an innovation incorporates aspects of all dimensions. Companies innovate to compete, grow and prosper, but profit is only part of the picture. Companies have the opportunity to be innovators by being visionaries who are motivated by a desire to improve that picture, whether it is for social, environmental, aesthetic, or personal reasons. By focusing on the big picture and innovating intelligently, companies can generate the profits they seek, develop a loyal company culture and have a positive impact on society.

What are you doing within your company to create a shared perspective on what innovation means? Overcoming the tendency to see the world from an egocentric perspective and appreciating the perspective of others is the first step in achieving organizational alignment with what the company is striving to achieve when they launch innovation initiatives.

Perspective: Paradigm--Company Innovation Mission and Vision for Sustaining the Core While Building for Innovation

Successful companies are able to balance themselves on the continuum of sustaining past and present success (preserve the status quo) while simultaneously harnessing the tremendous energy released by changing the way they do business. Changing too fast or too slowly has destroyed companies. Finding the right balance between risk and reward is crucial for success, if not survival. The perspective taken by the company shapes how they look at themselves as an organization, as well as how they view their employees, customers, and the relationships that bind them together in the marketplace.

One way to represent the challenge of balancing current and future success is to consider the difference between an organization working toward exploiting understood ways and one that is exploring new ways.[6]

Companies need to simultaneously focus on sustaining and building on the core business (the *what is* and *known knowns*) while at the same time focusing on identifying what the next step should be (the *unknown knowns*). The future end of the continuum is about *what could be*, a realm filled with *unknown unknowns*. Spend less time dealing with *what is*, and more time creating *what could be*. To leverage innovation effectively, realize that the rules for sustaining a core business

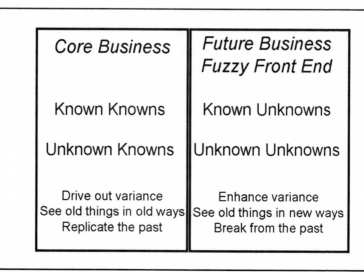

Core Business	Future Business Fuzzy Front End
Known Knowns	Known Unknowns
Unknown Knowns	Unknown Unknowns
Drive out variance See old things in old ways Replicate the past	Enhance variance See old things in new ways Break from the past

Figure 3.1

are very different from the rules for identifying and developing innovations and bringing the fuzzy front end of future business into focus. Just as importantly, evaluate core competencies and organizational processes to ensure that they are in alignment with intentions to innovate. For example, Toyota has processes in place to capture ideas on a continuous basis to achieve their innovation goal of always doing better. Companies such as IBM had to transform themselves to achieve their goal of doing things differently because they did not have the appropriate core competencies and capabilities to achieve their goal: moving from a hardware to a services company.[7]

The role of a good leader is to create an organizational climate, mindset, and tone that support both innovation and the core business operations in parallel. Proctor and Gamble has shown that it is possible to manage and balance the challenges of a large organizational culture that has to deal with innovation and sustaining business.[8] A company actively managing the balance between efficiency and innovation is perennial innovator 3M, which is in the midst of serious soul-searching about their culture, post-Six Sigma transformations.[9]

As leaders carefully assess where the transformational opportunities are, it is critical to root out the insidious assumption that innovation has to be something totally different; help employees recognize that simple changes can deliver significant value. UPS redesigned its delivery routes so that drivers minimize left turns (right turn only routes). This simple change cut thirty million miles and saved three million gallons of gas in 2007 by reducing the amount of time trucks idled and waited at traffic lights to turn left. This reduced UPS truck emissions by 32,000 metric tons of emissions (equivalent of 5,300 passenger cars) and made the roads safer for UPS drivers and other motorists by reducing the number of times trucks have to face and cross traffic. This shows how a simple, "do better" change can benefit the company, customers, and society.[10]

Companies need to be ambidextrous. For more details on how to create an "ambidextrous organization" that balances the needs of the core business while defining the future, refer to O'Reilly and Tushman (2002).[11]

Perspective: Process

"If you can't describe what you are doing as a process, you don't know what you're doing," said W. Edwards Deming. Processes typically evolve over time through experience and learning by doing, observing and, in some cases, through serendipity, with the express intent of achieving some sort of end. Toyota has been able to take advantage of a process improvement culture to deliver quality, performance, and value to a variety of customers across geographies with their Scion, Toyota, and Lexus brands, while at the same time maintaining high profits through operational excellence.

In some instances process innovations are totally hidden from the eyes of the customer yet is the secret sauce that leads to products and services full of customer benefits. "Processes are the stuff in the proverbial 'black box,' the alchemy unseen by consumers or inelegantly termed 'end users'…Yet all of these products, iPhone, Intel chips, and Google search engine—much acclaimed for their creativity—depend on obscure process innovations that, while highly complex and lacking glamour, are an essential part of the establishing a winning edge in commercial electronics." (Pascal Zachary, 2007)[12]

In other situations, process innovations are the basis of a new customer experience. Patricia Seybold, an expert on customer-centric management, observed: "Few companies have bothered to look carefully at the broad context in which customers select, buy, and use products and services. They've focused so much on fine-tuning their own offerings that they've failed to see how those products and services fit into the real lives of their customers."[13] Hammer (2004) describes *operational innovation,* where companies create entirely new ways of doing work, fundamentally different than the existing modes of operation, to deliver customer benefits, while at the same time benefiting the company by leveraging its competence and capabilities. It's not just doing the same thing better; it's doing business differently than the competition, which benefits the customer, and of course, the company. Hammer noted how Progressive Insurance stayed ahead of competitors by delivering value to customers through a process improvement that helped customers compare Progressive's rates with three competitors through a 800 number or website service. This service attracted potential customers and generated good will for Progressive.[14]

Another part of the insurance process that Progressive improved for customers, while helping themselves, was their claims process. Progressive changed the claims process by giving adjusters greater control to resolve claims. Adjusters are able to examine the car, prepare the estimate and, when possible, write a check on the spot for the claim rather than having to consult a central claims processing office. Customer benefits include quicker service with less hassle, which increases customer satisfaction and customer retention. Progressive has been able to identify and transform two critical areas in the insurance process profitably (1) obtaining insurance and (2) dealing with the unenviable event of actually having to file a claim and making it less painful.

Managers need to keep in mind how the process innovation will benefit the customer directly and/or indirectly and then determine the benefits to the company with a particular focus on the best way to positively differentiate the experience for the customer. For example, the core value of the Build-A-Bear Workshops is the experience of the process of building your own Teddy Bear while the process of fixing your own car is generally not seen as a customer experience enhancement.

Companies typically have process improvement initiatives going on throughout their organization in different departments, different business units, and at different levels. The question is: Is it possible to view all these processes at the same time, and identify the opportunities that others miss? It is possible, but the first step is to be aware of what is going on and then to recognize that the term "process" means different things to different people. The key is to view process comprehensively and at various levels of abstraction, from both the customer and company perspectives. There are various levels wherein the process can be evaluated.

Value Chain-What are the activities?

The overarching process to consider is the concept of the value chain, which describes the primary stages of the product life cycle from a product's invention/conception to the sale of a finished product as well as service and maintenance after final distribution. This includes all business activities in support of the product or service, including procurement and human-resource management. For example, Philips took different approaches in China and India based on its understanding of how these countries differ in terms of culture and available infrastructure. Because of the differences between China and India, Philips used different business models in each country, and adapted its value-chain activities accordingly. Philips focused on two dimensions of the value chain: how to distribute their products and, to a lesser extent, what products it makes. In China, eighty percent of Philips's consumer electronics products are sold in big-box stores similar to Best Buy in major cities such as Shanghai. The focus in China is on the few consumers with lots of money. In India, most of Philips' consumer sales come from 35,000 small, family-owned stores in urban areas and through three hundred distributors who drive vans on dirt roads and sell lower-cost hand-crank radios and starter televisions. Thus, the sales focus in India is on selling products to many consumers who don't have much money to spend. In the medical arena, it is a similar approach, selling high-end medical equipment to the Chinese government, while focusing its high-end sales on the private-hospital market and equipping vans to provide $2.25 x-rays and $10 pre-natal tests to people in remote rural areas of India.[15]

Value Networks

Value networks (or value webs) are, according to Wikipedia, "the human and technical resources in a business that work together to form relationships and add value to a product or service." The value network provides a frame of reference through which firms view their business environment, including their supplier, and channel partnerships as well as their competitors. This affects how they behave when executing their business strategy. Psychologically, companies and even their competitors can be lulled into complacency. They unwittingly start to operate as if the rules of the game, the players, and the teams they play against will always be the same. This mentality of assuming the status quo leads to what Peter Schwartz (2003) calls inevitable surprises, and Clayton Christensen refers to as the Innovator's Dilemma, whereby companies and established industries are overtaken by new competitors and technologies.[16] [17] Companies need to invest resources in new solutions for tomorrow's customers, as well as actively developing business relationships to meet tomorrow's challenges.

Customer Experience

What we call the customer experience begins with the customer's initial exposure through purchase of the product/service, to troubleshooting, maintenance, and service—all the touch points where the customer has an interaction with the offering. The customer experience should be as seamless as possible, and the relationships in the value network should be visible to outsiders only when such transparency provides actual customer value. Corporations often create separate internal organizations and/or developed partnerships with other companies to deal with different parts of the customer experience in the hopes of remaining competitive and optimizing their operations. The problem is that sometimes the customer experience suffers. Can you think of a recent purchase decision where it was obvious you were being bounced around like a Ping-Pong ball? "Sorry, but you have to call department X between 9:00 and 5:00." Or, "We are not responsible for service for this product. You will have to call company X." Or, "We sell you the product, but someone else handles delivery issues. If you want to log a complaint, you will have to call ... because our department does not handle that part of the process." When all is said and done, customers care little about internal company operations. Plain and simple, customers care about getting their needs met through a quality product and good service.

Interaction/Activity Flow

The process of a customer's experience with a product, service, or event can be deconstructed into various levels. Many analysis techniques are available, and various general terms have been used to describe these techniques, such as scenarios, use cases, and task analyses. However expressed, the interaction/activity flow describes the nuts-and-bolts interaction between a customer and a product or service as well as the customer's goals and expectations. All of these approaches share a common objective: understanding the activities or tasks (both behavioral and cognitive), as well as the information and resources required, for a customer to achieve their goal. What is it like to set up and use a home entertainment center? What is the perceived complexity, usability, and effort required to use it? What are the time and steps required to reach the intended goal?

Managers need to be aware and align process improvement efforts to ensure that the outcome is an improved customer experience that also benefits the company.

Perspective: Positioning

When people talk about innovation and business strategy, they inevitably use the term *market*. It's a deceptively simple but important term, and the vagueness with which it is generally used is remarkable.

"We need to increase our market penetration."
"We need to enter emerging markets."
"The marketplace is crowded."
"What is the market potential?"
"How are we and our competitors positioned in the market?"

If you try to define what the market is, you will quickly discover what a loosely understood term it is. According to Merriam-Webster Online (http://www.m-w.com) a market is defined as "an opportunity for selling, or the available supply of, or potential demand for, specified goods or services." This definition implicitly assumes three meanings:

- It relates to where the activity takes place;

- It includes the vendor who provides or supplies the goods and services to be purchased;

- It includes the customers who participate in the activity.

When people talk about the market, they usually refer to a combination of these meanings and assume that the distinctions

are obvious to everyone. That is a misleading assumption, however – one likely to lead to confusion and misunderstanding if
not clarified. Let us try now to provide some of that clarification.

At its simplest unit of analysis, a market can be defined as
the relationship between a single buyer and a single seller engaged in a transaction. The market as a context, or the environment in which the activity takes place, was once a much easier
concept to grasp because the term had a definite meaning. At
one time, the goods and services available in the market were
physically tangible and geographically constrained. The "market"
was a physical place where people congregated, where goods
were bought and sold, and where the public mercantile establishment was housed. Evidence of the importance of this physical
location in earlier historical times can be seen in the way various
European towns and cities were named. A notable example is the
town of Chipping Camden in England; *chipping* is the Old English
word for *market,* and the physical structure of the bustling marketplace once located there is still preserved. In Brussels, Belgium,
the central market square is an architectural marvel wherein the
business establishment and goods/services buildings have been
preserved, and its name—*de Grote Markt* in Flemish and *Grand
Place* in French—reflects the fact that it was once the location of
the market, and that it served an important purpose.

In the "good old days," customers traveled to the town's
market square and examined the available merchandise. The
vendors tried to attract customers with entertaining banter,
shouted out the availability of sudden bargains (the original
"blue light special") and proposed barter deals on the spot.
Vendors even tried to prove that their product was the best
compared to the competition by offering free samples, an
early example of *positioning.* Customers then perused what
was available at the marketplace and purchased what they
needed – meat, seafood, eggs, fruit, vegetables, bread, etc.
-- based on what they perceived was the best value, what they
planned to serve for meals, and how much money they wanted
to spend. Such bustling activity can still be seen at places such

Figure 3.2

as Pike Place Market in Seattle, where vendors are continually trying to attract attention by barking at passersby, tossing fish around, and offering free samples.

The whole concept of what the market is has become more difficult for companies to grasp because the physical market is no longer as direct, immediate, or tangible. For the most part, the days of real, intimate interactions and transactions between a buyer and seller are gone. In the contemporary marketplace, the chances are quite high that a customer and vendor will have little or no interaction beyond the product or service being provided. In spite of the movement toward "being green", we often don't repair and re-use things,– we just throw them away and buy new items. As civilization has progressed and transportation of goods and services has expanded to the point where there are almost no boundaries or geographic constraints, the notion of a market has become abstract. Relatively few transactions take place in a well-defined marketplace in the physical sense. The buyer and seller can be on opposite sides of the world and often are. Thus, the **concrete**, physical, local marketplace where seller and buyer know each other personally, the product was produced and used in the same locale, and everyone shared common cultural beliefs, norms, and values has dramatically changed. The feedback loop in today's marketplace is not immediate because of the number of intermediaries involved at the front, middle, and end of the transaction between the buyer and seller. Ironically, efforts have been made to portray the future of marketing as one in which companies will create intimate, one-to-one markets with customers, which in essence re-creates an old-fashioned marketplace.

The key point to grasp is that people tend to use the term "market" as if it is still a physical location where two individuals complete a transaction for goods and services in a personal manner, but the concept no longer matches reality. Today's marketplace is much more complex. In conversation, the disparity between concrete and abstract notions of the marketplace can cause confusion, because the people who are talking no longer share the same underlying assumptions about what "the market" really is. Companies can end up producing products consumers don't want. Customers can have expectations that aren't met. Competitors who better understand the customer's needs can swoop in and fill the gap. Indeed, miscommunication between a company and its customers can be expensive and damaging, so it's essential to prevent this from happening.

It is critical for people to spend the time making sure that everyone's underlying assumptions are the same. We recommend that companies draw out a detailed picture of who their customers really are, the relationships between companies, and the context in which the customers live in order to form a clearer understanding of the market under discussion. That way, companies will be better equipped to identify the key success factors and barriers that must be surmounted for a product/service to be successful in a particular niche.

The next time the "M" word comes up in a discussion, take a moment to clarify what everyone involved means as they use the term. When people talk in general terms about customers, markets, and products/services, listen carefully and ask more detailed questions about what they are really saying.

The value of clarifying and agreeing on a shared alignment about the market in terms of who the customers are and how they should be communicated to can lead to significant value. For example, Apple has positioned itself well and created a user experience that spans the range of user touch points. From interactions with their products to the purchasing and support process, each complements the other to create a "complete" and "perfect" experience. Apple has demonstrated that clear positioning and investment in the customer experience can result in a high ROI. Specifically, they have created a company store experience that attracts customers and gets them to purchase products. For example, Apple stores annual revenue per square foot of space is more than six times the revenue per square foot of Neiman Marcus, four times that of Best Buy, and about one and a half times that of Tiffany's.[18]

Perspective: Product/Services

The first place people head when they think of innovation is to products--automobiles, iPods, electricity, airplanes. Service innovation is an area of growing focus for corporation, government, and academic institutions (Service Research and Innovation Initiative-- www.thesrii.org/). Part of the challenge of achieving alignment is that everyone naturally jumps to solutions such as products and services and misses opportunities to look at innovation holistically. Individuals and groups tend to focus on different aspects of a product or service (e.g., infrastructure, applications, customer interfaces and interactions) depending on what they know or believe is most important (silos of focus). Discussions focus on the actual visible interactions and experiences because they are concrete. The problem lies in the fact that different people talk about products and services from different perspectives and thus are not communicating effectively; one person talks about available infrastructure while someone else is talking about user interface. Product, and to a lesser extent service innovation, is the typical perspective that companies feel the most comfortable in discussing because it is the most concrete. However, there is great opportunity in the ability to balance all perspectives to see where the most value can be created for the customer and the company.

The bottom line is that human psychology drives people's perception and action, so it is essential to have a common vision or strategy. Without a common understanding, all parts of the organization are essentially set up against each other, creating a creative stalemate and frustration.

Manager Key Takeaways

Achieving alignment is worth the effort: Simply being creative and generating and identifying new ideas isn't enough; *innovation* is about taking ideas and transforming them into action. For innovations to be successful both creativity and invention must be aimed toward the goal of making something real and tangible that improves people's lives and culture. However, creativity without focus is chaos; therefore, spending the time upfront to ensure alignment is invaluable. Key questions that managers need to answer:

Meaning of Innovation

- What do we (not I) mean when we say we need to innovate?

- Is it possible to create greater customer value by looking at the other 4P areas and seeing if we can optimize the customer experience by manipulating another area? For example, by improving the process of purchasing songs with iTunes Apple created significantly more customer value than the iPod alone.

Take the perspective of the customer and the company.

- Are we really taking the perspective of the customer's experience when we develop our strategy, or are we actually only taking care of ourselves as a company?

- How do we create mutual benefits for the customer and for us?

Paradigm: Balancing act between game changing and sustaining the core

- Have we created a vision that allows us to sustain our current success and encourage innovation for the future?

- Do we have the core competencies and capabilities to achieve our goals? Is our innovation focus on "doing better," "doing different," or "doing really different?"

Process: It's always there, but at what level?

- Is there customer value in the process itself or does it just enable value to be created?

- Do we have awareness and agreement on what level and areas of "process" should be focused on and those that will have the greatest positive impact for customers and the company? For example, is it in the product acquisition and customer service phases that the customer pain exists? What part of the task flow within customer service creates the greatest customer usability and dissatisfaction issues? Is it being forwarded to multiple people in the problem escalation process?

Market: What is it and who are the customers we hope to engage?

- Are we really talking about the same thing when we use the term "market?" Consider whether we focus too much on current customers when the real opportunity is going after new customers.

Products/Services: It's easy to focus on concrete products.

- If we are a product-oriented company, have we explored how services can extend the customer experience? Could services become the moneymakers of the future for a product-oriented company? Services are an under-explored and under-appreciated area of innovation that major companies are now teaming up to pursue. What about a service company looking for products that can support the service?

- Have we explored how to use combinations of products and services to extend customer experiences while at the same time creatively looking at how to make money?

- What are we doing to force ourselves to think differently so we don't fall into the trap of only creating incremental improvements?

Once a common understanding has been established, it's time to identify what barriers lay between a good idea and a successful innovation.

Chapter 4

**Forget about "marketing" to your customers:
Let personal experience sell your
offering for you**

*"The aim of marketing is to know and understand the
customer so well that the product or service fits him
and sells itself."*

~Peter Drucker

Suppose you are asked to spearhead a major product or service launch for your company. How do you proceed? How do you get the world to pay attention to your innovation? A common approach is to devote a great deal of energy and money to marketing and advertising to capture the customer's attention. According to Nielsen Media Research, the top-ten corporate advertisers spent nearly $4 billion in advertising in the first quarter of 2004 alone.[1] Sanford C. Bernstein & Co. estimates that by 2010, marketers will spend $27 billion on cable, $22.5 billion on the Internet, $19.1 billion on network television, and $17.4 billion on magazine ads.[2]

Companies are making assumptions about how people think and act when they throw significant amounts of money into marketing and advertising campaigns. Typical marketing theory starts with an assumption based on the psychological principle called *enrichment*.[3] In the words of William James, the world is a mass of chaotic sensations or a "bloomin', buzzin' confusion" that needs to be made sense of by the human mind. This perspective emphasizes that people need to make sense of incoming information about products/services through a logical decision-making process, not unlike a computer that does a lot of processing, organization, and interpretation to create meaning.

Most companies expend a great deal of energy (through advertising, marketing, etc.) building awareness for their offerings and trying to make them appealing and memorable to customers. The premise of advertising is to paint a favorable and convincing picture of the benefits of the offering, in essence defining the customer's experience for them. The fallacy of this approach is that it attempts to substitute an advertising executive's fantasy for the customer's reality. As Orvel Ray Wilson, co-author of the *Guerrilla Marketing* series put it: "Customers buy for their reasons, not yours." Curiously, even though the customer's *actual experience* with an offering is what is most likely to persuade them to buy it, this step in the adoption process is usually treated as an afterthought. Instead, the traditional marketing approach emphasizes persuading customers to *think* favorably about a product in the hope that they might try it. (See Figure 4.1)

From this approach, until and unless the customer tries the product or talks to someone else who has tried the product, the focus is on spending resources on the front-end process, attracting the customer's attention and finding ways of influencing the customer to decide the offering is worth trying. Regardless

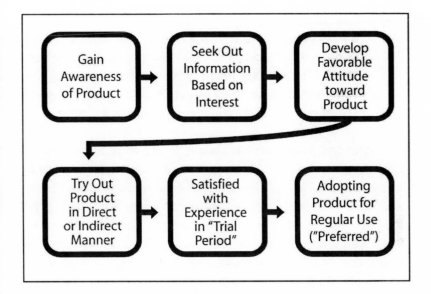

Figure 4.1

of how the message is delivered, all advertising is designed to create a strong association between the offering and the hypothetical value it will provide that persuades the customer to try it. Typical techniques most companies use to attract consumer attention include:[4]

- Using facts, figures, features, benefit statements, and specifications that build the case for the product and convince people that it's worth a try.

- Repeating the message so often that people can't forget it.

- Associating the product with a compelling, shocking, or humorous image. Funny mascots such as AFLAC's duck, GEICO's gecko and Nasonex's bee are examples.

- Grabbing customers' imagination by creating an image in their minds of how the product will transform their lives. Beer commercials that imply that drinking a particular beer will attract beautiful people.

- Using a credible or celebrity spokesperson the customer will recognize, and with whom the customer would like to be associated (e.g., Tiger Woods, Michael Jordan, Maria Sharapova, Peyton Manning). This strategy also implies that some of the person's skills or charisma will somehow rub off on you if you purchase the product.

Companies are now engaged in an advertising arms race, competing with each other to get customers' limited attention. Today, there is an explosion of mediums such as Internet, newsprint, radio, video games, satellite radio, cell phones, DVD players, movies, and computers by which customers are inundated with information. Furthermore, customers have greater control over the information they receive and can quickly tune out advertising that they see as "noise." Is there a better way to spend time, energy, and resources and increase customer acceptance and adoption? Yes. While advertising creates awareness for an offering, it is not the best way to persuade customers to actually *purchase and adopt* an offering. As consultant Patricia Seybold observed: "Companies spend a lot of time and money fine-tuning their relationships with customers. But those relationships don't exist in a vacuum." Our approach provides a way for companies to differentiate themselves from the competition.

James Gibson (1986) proposed that people can directly perceive the benefits of what is available in the environment through experience. He described a concept called an affordance that is the "fit [adaptation] between an animal's [person's] capabilities and the environmental supports and opportunities (both good and bad) that make possible a given activity."[5, 6] Essentially, Gibson is saying that the environment provides ample information about what it provides to people without a lot of mental processing and analysis. In other words, the environment, which includes products/services, communicates directly about how it can meet people's needs and people are actively seeking ways to meet their needs and improve their lives. The knife communicates to customers how it should be held, whether the grip will be firm, and that the blade is sharp enough to cut. If a product is designed correctly, and customers have an opportunity to interact with it, they should be able to determine almost immediately if it meets their practical and emotional needs to the point that they are motivated to purchase it. Thus, if given the opportunity, people discover potential uses for objects on their own based on how they experience the product/service directly, as opposed to having a product's features and benefits *explained* to them through an advertisement or brochure.

A customer's experience with an offering speaks far louder than anything the company can say about it in advertising or marketing, it's the "try it before you buy it" strategy. In fact, the typical way of marketing actually limits the customer's ability to personally identify and experience the benefits of a product. The experience is what differentiates the offering in a customer's mind. For example, at Pike Place Market in Seattle, Washington, produce salespeople offer free samples of exotic fruits and jellies. By giving the customer an opportunity to discover the value of the product -- by putting it in their mouths -- they are also sending a message to the customer that they believe in the quality of their product. Appliance manufacturers allow customers to discover the benefits of their products by trying them out at the showroom. This includes running dishes through the dishwasher, washing soiled clothes, and baking cookies in the oven. If the product delivers benefits to the customer and the experience is positive (e.g., easy to use or tasty), the marketing is easy because the product will practically sell itself! If the benefits of a product are real, and the customer discovers them, they will buy it. The more directly companies can assist customers in this process, by having customers' experience the offering, the better.

The implication of taking this approach is that it turns the traditional adoption process on its head, bypassing the costly and time-consuming assumptions that customers need to logically come to the conclusion that they are willing to even try an offering after going through a series of analysis steps. This approach assumes that if customers are given an opportunity to experience products and services firsthand – rather than secondhand through advertising or word of mouth – they are more likely to purchase and adopt an offering if the experience is a satisfying one. (Figure 4.2 shows the acceptance and adoption process from the "try it before you like it" (differentiation) approach as opposed to the traditional marketing (enrichment) approach.)

The bottom line is that if we involve all of a customer's senses through firsthand targeted exposure and interaction, we can make the benefits of the offering totally self-evident.

The nuances and complexity of human psychology make it difficult for companies to develop products that please a wide range of people. Consequently, guessing what customers want is a losing game. Engaging customers early and often in the development process eliminates a tremendous amount of expensive guesswork. As we mentioned earlier, people tend to think concretely rather than abstractly and hypothetically, which explains why people tend to have greater difficulty articulating what they want when discussing in the abstract. Customers can co-create, evolve, evaluate and advise companies on how to develop a solution that meets their needs, but they have to see and touch it first so they can provide feedback on what works and what doesn't. Customers that have something concrete to respond to will provide more useful feedback than customers who are asked to speculate in the abstract about a product's or service's potential benefits. This approach, anchored in the concrete and tangible, provides companies with an early warning process to determine whether a given solution will succeed, and what needs to change to reduce risk and ensure adoption. When a company's processes are responsive to the true voice of the customer all along the line, from conception to marketing and fulfillment, that company is much less likely to fall into the many psychological traps that can stop the momentum of an innovative idea in its tracks. A complementary innovation strategy focuses

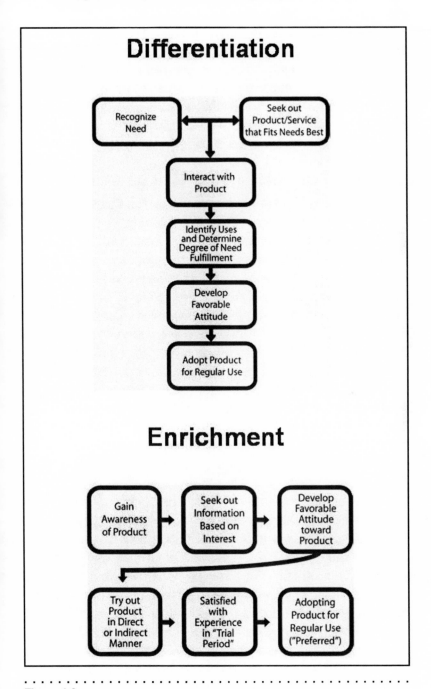

Figure 4.2

on the interaction with the offering early and often throughout development with an emphasis on customer experience design.

A shift from the traditional marketing approach to a customer experience-driven approach requires managers to change their perspective from focusing on what is going on in the customer's head to the environmental context in which the customer resides and his/her experience of the environment.

Customer Feedback and Concept Discovery

Most companies believe they are "customer-focused," "customer-centric," or that they are listening to the "voice of the customer." Unfortunately, in many instances, the primary source of customer feedback is verbal feedback obtained out of context. The trouble is, customers don't always know what they want, aren't always able to articulate it, and are often unreliable reporters, even of their own experiences. Neuroscience researcher Steven Pinker calls this phenomenon the "baloney generator."[7] Neuroscientists have observed that people are amazingly adept at generating false explanations of their behavior. For example, people tend to give more weight to recent experiences, good or bad, than more distant memories. The human mind isn't a video recorder; we tend to exaggerate, generalize, diminish, or distort memories based on past experiences, cognitive biases, and personal filters (as discussed earlier). Thus, customers filter their experiences and recount what they believe they are doing, and often may not even know why they behave the way they do, which makes accurate and complete recall nearly impossible. This is why asking customers what they think – and believing what they say – can be extremely misleading. For example, when workers in a large petrochemical plant were asked to describe how they completed each task, they recited the procedure in the handbook or used generalizations such as: typically, usually, and generally. When watched, however, they actually used all kinds of shortcuts and workarounds, such as sticking Post-it-note memory aids all over the place, which were not part of the official procedure. Were they lying? No. They were just recounting what they *believed* they were doing.

The problem is that companies fall into the psychological trap of assuming customers are able to accurately articulate their needs and experiences and thus become reactive to incoming customer feedback. They prioritize customer feedback based on inappropriate criteria, such as assigning more significance to the most recent feedback, or giving a preferential bias toward feedback from their most important, largest, or loudest customer. One or two angry e-mails about an offering can often attract the attention of upper management, even if there are millions of silent customers who are perfectly happy with the offering. These "squeaky wheels" often exert undue influence in the decision-making process and skew things in directions they might not otherwise go.

The focus on the "squeaky wheels" creates an innovation paradox that reinforces the tendency for companies to create *incrementally improved* products/services rather than ones that are completely new in concept and design, because the customer feedback usually supports the status quo. Remember that customers tend to operate in the concrete, which means they will voice concerns and complaints about what they don't like about the current solution and how they would improve it.

Given that it's hard for people to talk accurately about what they think they know, it's doubly difficult for them to speak meaningfully about what they don't yet know – for instance, what life might be like with a fabulous new product or service. Companies need to shift their approach from simply asking customers about what they need from within the four walls of their offices, to "going out into the wild" and carefully and unobtrusively observing customers in their natural habitat.

Immersion in the customer environment, and direct observation of what is going on, allows companies to: determine customers' true behavior patterns and generates insights into the barriers and limitations of current solutions; verify whether customers behave the way they *say* they do; obtain a fuller picture of the customer's environment; and – most important of all – help identify unanticipated opportunities that no one could have guessed, even if you asked them. Thus, rather than transient and short-lived exposure to customers, spend more time living and breathing the life of the customer to gain an appreciation of their specific environment. For example, if you manufactured wheelchairs, it would be useful to follow wheelchair users for periods of time. Better yet, it might be a good idea to live the life of a person in a wheelchair for a time to understand the experience and understand how to better serve those customers. Proctor and Gamble formalized this process into their organizational DNA with consumer immersion programs called "Living It" and "Working It." "Living It" is a program where employees have the opportunity to live with consumers for several days, so they can fully experience day-to-day activities and decisions made by customers at home, work, and play. "Working It" is a program where employees have the opportunity to work behind the counter of a store so they can obtain insight into why customers buy or do not buy a product in the store, and how their design, packaging, and shelving decisions either support or hinder purchase decisions.[8]

This is where companies can identify opportunities that even customers do not realize they are missing, which is where true innovation comes from. Generally speaking, if someone can tell you about an innovation, it has already been discovered and is therefore not new.

Real insight comes from being an astute observer of the world around you. This includes observation of current and potential customers as well as the general environment. The point of this approach is that the world is filled with information, insight, and discovery--if you are willing to look for it. Marcus Aurelius said, "Nothing has such power to broaden the mind as the ability to investigate systematically and truly all that comes under thy observation in life," while Vera Rubin said, "Science progresses best when observations force us to alter our preconceptions." The goal is to avoid falling into the traps of the status quo and a single egocentric view of the world.

There are many approaches for conducting effective observational research for which there are training experts and consultants; however, here are a few tips that will help present a comprehensive picture of the environment and build stakeholder buy-in within your organization:

- **Broaden Your Perspective; Narrow Your Focus:** Becoming a *fly on the wall* can be overwhelming due to the desire to identify key behaviors and observations at the same time that a whole stream of complex human behavior is coming at you. Try observing the customer's environment in a structured manner that starts with no intervention whatsoever and becomes gradually more structured as patterns emerge, and links to socially, behaviorally, or historically important factors become apparent. The structure provides a balance between focus and creativity that reduces observer bias while still identifying new and previously unobserved opportunities.

- **Diversity of Observers:** Given that people have individual and group filters on how they see the world, it is critical to have a variety of people involved in observing customers and their environment. As pointed out earlier, companies such as Philips Electronics and Motorola employ anthropologists, technologists, sociologists, psychologists, musicologists, and graphic designers, along with experts in typical functional areas such as marketing, product planning, and development. It is useful to utilize uninitiated observers who are new to the company and/or the industry because they generally don't come with a lot of historical legacy, bias, or baggage that leads to status quo thinking and constraints. Free of the past, they can ask the "why" question and perhaps see things differently.

- **Diversity of Users and Contexts:** When it comes to innovation it is important to observe beyond the typical core customers and customer environments and see what is going on in the fringes. For example, some have argued that there are sets of users called *lead users* who have needs that go far beyond what is currently available, and the goal is to identify and use them as customer innovators (Von Hippel, Thomke & Sonnack 1999; Thomke 2003).[9, 10] In essence, they precede everyone on the adoption curve, identifying emerging needs and creating the foundation for solutions, which the initial group of technology enthusiasts and innovators ultimately adopt for use. Companies need to adapt concepts to meet the needs and levels of expertise of a broader set of potential users, remembering that lead users are a unique and sometimes bizarre set of individuals. Going beyond the typical user contexts to see how they meet their needs and adapt to varied circumstances provides insight that is outside the expected. Going even further, identify key similarities or constraints that exist in other industries or situations to find out how they are solving problems. CEMEX, the concrete maker, found insight regarding the just-in-time delivery of ready cement to construction sites by observing how 911 operators deal with responding to an emergency that they cannot predict.[11]

- **Diversity of Uses; The Aha:** Observing how offerings are experienced in "real life" provides opportunities to see additional uses that customers have discovered that were not originally intended by the company. James Gibson observed how people see different possibilities at different times depending on their needs at the moment: "The fact that a stone is a missile does not imply that it cannot be other things as well. It can be a paperweight, a bookend, a hammer, or a pendulum bob."[12] People are always finding new ways to use products that the product's designers didn't intend. The trick is to identify these uses and take advantage of them. Look at all the uses of duct tape! Toothbrush manufacturers never intended for people to use them as tile-grout cleaners. 3M's Post-it Note has become ubiquitous with hundreds of different applications using the same adhesive on paper. The magazine *Real Simple* runs a column called "Solutions: New Uses for Old Things." Writers describe the original use for a product, an "Aha!" use (new use), and the reward (benefit of the new use). They are onto something that all companies should think about when they seek growth. What "Aha!" uses can you discover through observing your current or potential customers?

Prototyping: Make the future concrete for customers to respond to.

A challenge for innovators: the greater the difference between the new product/service concept from its previous solution, the more difficult it is for customers to appreciate how the concept will benefit and change their lives. In particular, when potential solution concepts move from familiar to unfamiliar territory, it becomes more difficult for customers to provide feedback because they begin to encounter things *they don't know they don't know*. This is because they do not have any experiential reference point (anchoring).

How do we resolve this issue? We recommend carrying out prototyping and usability evaluations early and often, so that customers can try out the product/service in a real-world scenario, and improvements can be made along the way. The goal of prototyping is to take the abstract and make it concrete by creating an initial characterization of the product/service that is suitable for evaluation—one that gives people a vision of how the product/service works, how it would affect the customer, and how it would fit into their environment. As Philips Electronics chief executive Gerald Kleisterlee said, "Design helps us bridge the gap between the present and the future and makes the future tangible today."[13] Steve Jobs said, "It's really hard to design products by focus group. A lot of times, people don't know what they want until you show it to them."[14]

Prototyping concepts in this way generate invaluable insights into how customers might interact with the product, and whether the product will really work. Prototypes allow the company to observe how customers might actually use and potentially become emotionally connected to the product/service experience, rather than simply asking customers to imagine what the experience might be like. Proctor and Gamble has incorporated prototyping into processes such as the "Innovation Gym." In the "Innovation Gym," ideas are prototyped early and often, and instant customer feedback can quickly identify ideas that seemed good conceptually but when prototyped and shown to customers are deemed "dogs" within a matter of days rather than months or years.[15]

In essence, this approach helps customers move from the *what is* to the *what could be,* and provides companies an opportunity to obtain reliable customer feedback along the way as well as develop potential advocates for the offering when it is ready to be launched. Following are some additional tips on effective prototyping:

- **"Eat your own dog food":**[16] It's important for companies to try for themselves what they want to sell to their customers. This makes it possible to identify the real "dogs" early on, and avoid wasting time and money developing bad ideas. For example, Philips asked one hundred top managers to spend a weekend trying to set up various Philips gadgets in their own homes. Many returned frustrated and angry. This allowed Philips managers to feel the pain their customers were feeling. In this case, unfortunately, the internal feedback was obtained after the products were released to customers. Obviously, if they had done this exercise during the concept-development phase, they would have done a few things differently.

- **Setting and staging the context and experience:** When staging a proposed customer experience, it's important to re-create, as realistically as possible, how a customer and product will interact. Otherwise, the data that comes from the experiment could yield mistaken conclusions. This is especially true for products that interact with or depend upon other products to work. For example, high-tech computing systems or home-entertainment systems interact with a variety of other equipment, so it's important to include those other devices in test scenarios. If you don't, you'll be ignoring factors that could have a huge impact on how customers experience your product.

- **Step out and accept the verdict of customers early and often:** Accept the verdict of customers with humility and admit failure: fail fast, fail often, and fail smart. Make no excuses and do not rationalize away what customers tell you just to make it easy for the company. Spend time figuring out why customers don't like the concept, redesign it to address the issues, and then retest it to see if the issues have been resolved. Leonardo da Vinci said: "Although nature commences with reason and ends in experience it is necessary for us to do the opposite, that is to commence with experience and from this to proceed to investigate the reason." Remember, if you don't eat humble pie early on, no amount of advertising makes up for poorly designed offerings and experiences. A company's worst enemies are dissatisfied customers because they tend to be highly motivated to share their negative experiences and pain, which creates significant negative buzz.

Marketing

Edwin Land said, "Marketing is what you do when your product is no good." His comment reinforces the point that marketing is often an afterthought activity wherein companies attempt to figure out how to persuade people that they need and want an offering through indirect advertising and other promotions. Of course, this plays right into the traditional marketing approach we have been discussing. Ideally, the marketing of an offering begins much earlier in the process than it typically does, and entails engaging customers from the outset by observing them and having them experience the concept offering early and often.

Build customer momentum through engagement with the offering and other users.

A shift in marketing is taking place wherein actual users are enlisted to actively be part of marketing a product rather than being passive receptacles and receivers of company advertising. Creating enthusiasts who have actually used the product or service can be more effective and less expensive than a broad-based advertising campaign. For example, advertising firms such as Big Fat Brain are engaging customers to create advertising for their clients. They created masterchiptheater. com for a potato chip maker called Grippo's where customers were encouraged to create commercials. Customers created potato chip-oriented commercials such as "Silence of the Yams" and "The Good, the Bag, and the Ugly."[17] Makers of Mentos candies did not know that if a packet of Mentos is dropped into a one-liter Coke bottle, the contents explode out of the bottle like a geyser. Customers clued them in to this novel use of the product, and the company now features a Mentos Geyser Contest prominently on its Web page (www.mentos.com), complete with customer videos posted on YouTube.

Enthusiastic, passionate evangelists can be a powerful influence on fence-sitters, pulling potential customers on the bandwagon and creating momentum. People who share experiences with others are often more believable and have more in common with the typical customer. People are more likely to try something new if they feel that those who they want to associate with are supporters. It is perceived as "cool."

Bring potential users to the next level of engagement and comfort so that they adopt.

Beyond engaging current customers as enthusiasts, companies can extend the power of this premise even further by helping customers "discover" the benefits provided by their products/ services. A concept called *scaffolding*, introduced by Russian psychologist Lev Vygotsky, describes how one person can help another move to the next level of skill mastery. Scaffolding is like building construction where the scaffold serves as a support around the building until construction is complete and the scaffold is no longer required.[18] The support and assistance can take the form of direct interaction between the *teacher* and the interested, motivated *student,* or by having the student indirectly observe the teacher and learn through imitation (observational learning). Consider home-improvement stores that offer hands-on courses for do-it-yourself projects or television shows like "This Old House." Of course, hands-on experiences with an instructor provide a greater degree of support, encouragement, and immediate opportunity to imitate the behaviors. In general, the more direct the experience, the more effective the scaffolding will be.

Design Through Observation

A great example of design where the focus is on the observation of customer behavior, with direct experience of the offering starting early in the design process, is the Alaska Airlines "Airport of the Future" project. Alaska Airlines used observational research and prototyping very effectively in designing the customer experience for airport passenger check-in at the airport terminal. The project's goal was to increase customer satisfaction and reduce wait times, while reducing Alaska Airlines' costs by increasing agent productivity, reducing terminal building costs, and reducing the need for agents by using technology (e.g., terminal kiosks and Internet check-in). Most striking is that the lines at the Alaska Airlines counter are typically no longer than three deep, and travelers are usually heading to the security line in eight minutes or less compared to the typical 20-30 minutes.[19]

The concept was developed by a cross functional team of employees who visited diverse venues outside the airline industry such as theme parks, hospitals, and retailers with similar procedures and processes (e.g., waiting in line and completing a transaction). This represents diversity in terms of the team as well as looking outside of the industry to see how others have solved a similar problem. The team brainstormed ideas based on their own experiences and then prototyped various designs, starting with low-fidelity designs using cardboard and progressing to complete designs. The designs were tested with real passengers and employees starting in a warehouse and validated in an actual airport. Now that the design has been validated, improved, and implemented in their Anchorage terminal, the goal is to replicate the design across their entire terminal system. Other airlines recognize the achievement and are working to copy Alaska's design. Some of the key findings from Alaska Airlines' observational, prototyping, and real-world experience:

- Strategically placing employees in key places of the check-in area associated with the check-in process reduces confusion, speeds up the check-in, and improves the customer experience. "Lobby coordinators" are right at the entry of terminal check-in (e.g., an idea incorporated from observing workers at Disney) to help people figure out what they want to do immediately and get them to where they need to go. Attendants are then available to assist and teach travelers how to use the kiosks to complete tasks such as getting boarding passes.

- Design of the physical space can optimize the experience such as having the agent between two baggage belts so they can help multiple people and not waste time hauling bags and walking extra steps, having the area arranged so passengers can clearly see security, and locating the kiosks in banks so passengers can quickly decide what they want to do and get to the task at hand.

- Redesigning the entire check-in process beyond the actual time in the terminal. Seventy-three percent of Alaska Airlines customers use the kiosk or the Internet for check-in as opposed to fifty percent for the rest of the airline industry. This reduces customer wait times and reduces Alaska Airlines costs related to agent time.

Manager Key Takeaways

- Spend less time talking to your customers about what you plan to create for them. Have you identified opportunities for customers to directly interact with potential offerings early and often?

- Spend time in the customer environment to discover what is really going on. People tend to focus on what is wrong with their current situation. Have you created opportunities to identify issues that customers aren't even aware of?

- Be sure to observe the customer environment with the broadest set of perspectives so that you gather the richest set of insights.

- Prototype and stage the customer experience as early and often as possible so that you can identify the best opportunities and get rid of the losers as early as possible.

- Marketing should be based on clearly identified customer benefits that can be experienced rather than on advertising based on enticement.

- Have you identified customer advocates that can help build momentum for the offering?

- What are you doing to support potential customers?

Chapter 5

Understanding Socio-Cultural Contexts

"Everything is connected … no one thing can change by itself."

~Paul Hawken

The late Gestalt psychologist Kurt Koffka (1935) offered this thought about the importance of context: "It has been said: The whole is more than the sum of the parts. It is more correct to say that the whole is something else than the sum of its parts, because summing is a meaningless procedure, whereas the whole-part relationship is meaningful."[1] To appreciate what Koffka meant, recall a fond memory of a great meal you had at a restaurant. In all likelihood it wasn't just the food that made the meal so special, it was the *ambience* or *atmosphere* of the event – the conversation, service, music, lighting, and everything else that contributed to your enjoyment, all of which resulted in a pleasurable experience.

These two terms – *ambience* and *atmosphere* – are the essence of context, and they are what innovators should try to create for their customers. The Merriam-Webster dictionary defines ambience as "a feeling or mood associated with a particular place, person, or thing," whereas *atmosphere* is defined as "a surrounding influence or environment or a dominant aesthetic or emotional effect or appeal."

As Koffka suggests, any given experience is a dynamic dance of elements that add up to much more than the sum of its parts. It's that extra something that interests us. True, the whole idea of "context" can seem like an amorphous blob. In trying to sort out what influences human behavior, we can identify many factors that affect us on a day-to-day basis, but no one is conscious of *all* factors at play in every moment of their life. The challenge is to understand and systematically identify how these factors, along with others, influence the customer's perception of an innovation and its ultimate purchase and adoption.

To create a superior customer experience, one with a sufficiently attractive *ambience,* all the surrounding environmental factors must support and extend the experience of the product/service. Such an approach not only surprises and delights customers, it gives product and service developers a better understanding of how various factors interact with each other. This puts them in a better position to predict how and why customers behave the way they do, and anticipate how and why certain innovations spread while others do not.

Contextual Resistance

In 1979, developmental psychologist Urie Bronfenbrenner came up with a model that can help us understand and systematically analyze or *diagnose* context.[2] He saw context as layers of socio-cultural "spheres of influence" that interact with each other. In his model the individual is surrounded by various outward-spiraling contexts – e.g, family, community, environment, culture, country, etc.— all of which influence the behavior of the individual. Bronfenbrenner's approach provides a way to make some sense out of the relative chaos of so many varied contextual factors. If one can determine how these "spheres of influence" are affecting customers, and then deduce how customers are likely to act, one can anticipate behavior patterns much more accurately.

Individual human differences matter when it comes to innovation, because innovation is an inherently human endeavor. In this model, **individuals'** willingness to embrace the change and disruption of innovation ranges from people who enthusiastically try almost anything just for the heck of it, to people who won't change for any reason. Thus, some people are willing to take risks and are open to change while others are not, and some people have the ability to influence others to change while others do not. These individual differences translate into different types of customers, and what is happening in their culture and environment can have a profound impact on their behavior. If the contextual force is strong enough, it can even make people do things they would not choose to do individually, such as eating a low-carb diet, or quitting smoking. How individuals perceive, respond and react to products and each other affects how customers and companies behave, which in turn affects the success or failure of any given innovation.

Surrounding the individual is the **immediate environment**—the settings, the people, and the physical objects with which the individual has direct contact. This includes the products that people use, their immediate family relationships and friends, the workplace, schools, churches, and any other setting with which they have direct contact. People do not evaluate new ideas in a vacuum; they are influenced by the people they know, the publications they read, the TV shows they watch, the radio stations they listen to. Without necessarily even being conscious of it, their behavior is influenced by the collective influence of these various points of social contact; so understanding when, where, how, and why certain individuals are drawn to certain contexts is important.

The **social and economic context** is the next sphere, and includes the broader social and economic situation in which the individual exists. A person's economic situation, good or bad, can profoundly affect the way they view the world, and certainly affects what people can buy. Where people grew up and where they currently live reflect their social/economic context. Money and social standing are tangible things that people can feel, largely because of the limitations involved. Rich people have access to resources, products, and power that poor people don't, and they behave very differently. Whether we want to admit it or not, how much money we make defines what we can and can't do, and is the prism through which we view much of the world around us.

Finally, the **cultural context** is the source of our ideas about what is "right" and "good," or what is required to live a "good life." It consists of the beliefs, values, and guidelines for our behavior in society. These cultural customs and norms influence initial purchase and adoption decisions in several ways, including our ideas about what it means to live the good life, and what it takes to achieve the American Dream. Is it a certain size of home, neighborhood, number and type of cars, computers, and televisions? These are all perceptions and expectations shaped by the cultural context in which we live. For a farmer in Africa, the good life might be half an acre of plowable land and a few healthy goats. To a stockbroker in Manhattan, however, that life might be considered a hellish existence, because his expectations are much different. Consider the model depicted in Figure 5.1.

Spheres of influence can be seen as social constraints or rules of engagement that serve as a scaffold, or foundation, for the activity of individual customers. The best way to understand a customer's context is from the inside out, from the personal biases and preferences brought to a purchasing situation, through all of the socio-economic and cultural contextual fac-

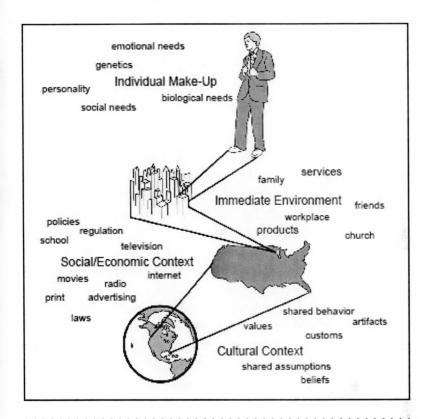

Figure 5.1

tors involved, and on into the details of how the customer interacts with the environment. People have some common goals
that they are all working toward (e.g., food, sleep, shelter), but
cultural influences affect the ways in which they achieve these
goals. These spheres of influence can be distant, such as culture, or direct, in the immediate environment and its link to the
individual customer. However, even if the immediate environment has a more direct and visible influence on the customer
than the outer cultural layers, the influence of the outer layers
should not be underestimated when it comes to innovation. For
example, governments and laws are part of everyone's cultural
context and influence how we behave, but they are not something most of us come into conflict with on a daily basis.

How does all of this relate to innovation? Well, a richer contextual perspective acts as a lens through which it is possible to observe spheres of influence in action, allowing us to discover new market opportunities and potential solutions that weren't visible before. For example, many opportunities can be discovered by paying close attention to emerging trends and closely observing people while they use existing products and services, then determining what is lacking or troublesome in those products. Our goal in this chapter is to suggest a method for distinguishing relevant socio-cultural factors from irrelevant ones, making it possible to gather valuable insights and turn them into a competitive advantage.

The Bugaboo stroller company came into being because one person paid close attention to several ongoing socio-cultural trends and found a solution for a problem he noticed. Over the past several decades, as more women have entered the workforce, more men have been staying home with the children to do childcare. A Dutch designer named Max Barenbrug noticed that even though more men were becoming involved in childcare, most of the equipment for doing this job was designed for women. In particular, Barenbrug noticed that the scale of most strollers forced men to bend over, or assume other uncomfortable positions in order to push their babies around. To solve this problem he invented a stroller with a telescoping handle. But stroller manufacturers rejected the idea. Undeterred, Barenbrug went on to create the Bugaboo stroller company, which is now considered the premium "must have" stroller for active, on-the-go families, particularly for fathers responsible for the daily care of babies and toddlers. The strollers themselves cost anywhere from $600 to $1,000, and are often referred to as "hip."[3]

Barenbrug was able to identify an opportunity in a mature market (baby strollers) and ended up developing a high-margin, must-have product within the subculture of stay-at-home dads. Perhaps most astonishing of all, he was able to take a baby stroller and make it "cool." Other such companies as DadGear and Diaper Dude are picking up on this trend, creating heavy-duty diaper bags and other traditional equipment in colors and materials that appeal to men, such as canvas and leather. What made these innovations possible was the way in which Bugaboo and other companies identified an underserved customer group (involved male parents) created by an emerging social trend – changing parental roles in society – and then created a product to fill the niche.

Contextual Factors That Affect the Customer

Bronfenbrenner's model provides a way to partition and analyze various contextual factors affecting products and customers. But in order to identify and execute on innovation opportunities, companies need to dig deeper to find out what factors will generate either resistance or attraction at each of the spheres of influence. These critical contextual factors need to be addressed: compatibility, social connectedness, and synchronicity:

- **Compatibility** with existing products/services/culture

- **Social connectedness** of the social structures supporting the product/service

- **Synchronicity** of the various layers of context

Compatibility

The force of resistance keeps things apart, but **compatibility** is how well things work in harmony. If you think about a customer's life as a kind of system that they have created to get along in the world, and if you think of products and services as part of the machinery that makes that system work, it should be apparent that customers are more likely to purchase products and services that are compatible with their lifestyle system. Compatible products and services generate more attraction than resistance. Products that "fit" into a customer's lifestyle – that is, ones that easily find their own context in a person's life – tend to get adopted, while those that don't fit – ones that generate too much resistance – do not get adopted.

Many products are developed without enough thought given to whether they have been designed for the needs, expectations, activities and worldviews of the market they are targeting. Attention to such details would increase their success rate considerably. For example, Apple's strategy of releasing a version of iTunes and an iPod compatible with Microsoft Windows® was a huge enhancement that enabled non-Apple users to adopt Apple's solution without having to scrap their current computer or buy a new one. Before that, customers literally had to buy a whole new system if they wanted to enjoy an iPod.

A roadblock innovators constantly face is that people often have a great deal of time and money invested in current solutions, and have become comfortable with these solutions to the point where the costs, aggravation of switching, and disruption to the overall familiar (not necessarily superior) customer experience prevents them from making the leap. Microsoft's Windows® operating system is a good example of this phenomenon. Windows® so dominates the operating system market that it is improbable that another operating system such as Linux or Apple or anything else – even if it is better -- will unseat it. Since competing with Windows is futile, the next best thing for companies that want to exist in the Windows universe to do is be compatible with it. This is why there are hundreds of software companies that survive and thrive through development partnerships with Microsoft. Even Apple hardware can now run the Windows operating system along with the Mac operating system.

Social Connectedness

Social connectedness is another factor that affects the acceptance and adoption of innovation. Social connectedness is a function of social, professional or commercial relationships wherein potential benefits and risks are shared. Companies do not exist in a vacuum; they are part of a dynamic web of activity involving hundreds or thousands of other companies that also supply various supplies and services. The strength and vitality of this network of relationships can make or break an innovation. Social connectedness influences both the customer and the industry, and together they each play a role in the adoption of new products and services. Social networks are particularly powerful with the use of cell phones, text-messaging, Internet message boards, blogs, and sites such as YouTube. Word of mouth can now travel farther and faster than ever, and profoundly influence whether customers and potential customers use your product or service. These networks are the life-blood of breakthrough ventures that create their own self-contained universe of enthusiastic customers. Out of nowhere contagious "viral" marketing campaigns can spring up. The burden is on the company to deliver a superior product or provide a compelling customer experience. Without it, social networks – the broadcasters of buzz -- can also hurt or even kill a company. That's why in addition to building a network of product evangelists and promoters, one must also try to minimize detractors. Detractors poison a social network by telling everyone they know how horrible the service was, or how they got ripped off.

Indeed, identifying and energizing an army of product evangelists is the most effective marketing program a company can use. The best "evangelists" are trusted, respected, credible, enthusiastic, positive, charismatic people who also happen to be committed believers and users of the product/service. Who should companies focus on when trying to identify these evangelists? *New Yorker* writer Malcolm Gladwell, in his 2002 book *The Tipping Point,* describes three types of individuals who are skilled at translating and communicating the message of the innovators and early adopters to the rest of us. These three types of people provide the fuel for change within a social network by providing different types of connective glue.[4] They serve as filters for extraneous information and tend to emphasize (and even exaggerate) critical information that affects behavioral change. They also possess a set of personal characteristics and resources that make them especially effective at fueling change in others. Three types of people that can provide the connective tissue for an innovation:

1. **Connectors:** People who provide social glue by collecting friends and acquaintances from different worlds, subcultures, and social niches. Connectors are social butterflies who like people, connect people across different boundaries, and enjoy observing the social world around them.

2. **Mavens:** Mavens are collectors of information who make connections between pieces of knowledge in interesting ways. More important, they are socially motivated to share the information because they truly want to use their knowledge to solve other people's problems.

3. **Persuaders:** Persuaders are great salespeople. They have high emotional intelligence and are able to persuade even the most skeptical people to try something new based on their advice.

If companies were able to identify and tap into the skills of these types of people and inspire them to become product promoters, think of the impact! For example, what if you could engage their skills in promoting a complementary innovation? You could start by getting the mavens to see how the complementary innovation provides a superior experience and have them share the message with the connectors and persuaders they know. Then leverage the network of connectors and bring along the persuaders to spread the enthusiastic message to a broad range of potential customers who have different levels of risk aversion and who reside in diverse customer niches.

Synchronicity

Synchronicity happens when events occur or mesh at the same time, which leads to a convergence of factors that makes things fall into place, as if they were meant to be. Synchronicity doesn't just have to be a surprise, however – it can be tracked, planned for, and even influenced by looking for contextual alignments that make synchronous activity more likely.

Synchronicity isn't as mysterious or mystical as it sounds. It happens all around us because events in the real world are connected through time. Indeed, it can be said that most innovations themselves are products of synchronicity – a serendipitous alignment of ideas, people, resources, and needs or desires that leads to something marketable. For example, XBox Live could not exist without several other technological factors falling into place, such as a broad high-speed Internet infrastructure, computer chips and processors capable of handling sophisticated graphics, armies of game-hungry young people, etc. As a product, XBox Live can be seen as a vortex of synchronicity that brought these disparate technological elements together into a cool, fun, revolutionary activity. Take away any of these elements and the synchronous beauty of the idea falls apart, which is why so many previous attempts at enticing large audiences to participate in online gaming faltered.

Often, when developing truly innovative ideas, parts of the synchronicity puzzle are in place, but ones that would make the idea marketable are not. The idea either dies in R&D or those working on it wait until more of the critical elements are in place. Alternative automobile fuel technologies such as battery-operated cars are at that point right now: they exist, and can be produced, but the market conditions aren't quite right for wide deployment at the moment, and the right political context for them has yet to emerge out of the global angst over oil supplies. However, demand for battery-operated, hybrid and alternative-fuel automobiles are on the rise, and all the elements are beginning to fall into place for them to become a mainstream alternative to the combustion engine. Toyota, for one, is reaping the rewards of betting on hybrid technology and patiently investing in it over time until the contextual factors became aligned.

When surveying the socio-cultural landscape for signs of alignment and opportunities for synchronicity, the challenge is anticipating where there may be points of connection in the foreseeable future. Time is the most fluid and important factor in this analysis. People, products, companies, societies, and civilizations all move through time together, but evolve, develop and mutate at different speeds. So what should companies look for when assessing customer behavior in context and time as it relates to the acceptance and adoption of innovation?

- **Watershed Events:** What historical events have occurred in the customers' lifetime that makes a product/service successful at one point in time and not another? People born during the Great Depression tend to be more frugal and do not like to waste or discard things. The events of September 11 made people reflect on the purpose of their lives and affected their feelings of security. Innovators analyzing historical trends must assess how events unfolding today are likely to affect customer preferences for products and services tomorrow.

- **Life Phase:** What phase of life is the customer currently in? In many ways, the desire for particular products or services depends upon the age of the customer. College students do not go out and buy high-end leather furniture, for example, but aging empty nesters, who feel they've earned the right to splurge on comfort and luxury, do.

- **Product Maturity:** What is the phase of the product/service's maturity? As products mature, customers' perceptions and expectations of them change. People tolerate shortcomings in new products but not in products that have been around for a while. Some products withstand the test of time better than others, but almost all products must evolve and improve at some point, or risk becoming obsolete.

- **Win-Win Positioning:** Are there ways to position a product so that everyone wins? Cell-phone companies seem to have hit the mark with plans that offer phones for the whole family and free calling time for calls to family members or friends within the same network.

Parents can keep track of their children and not have to worry about high phone costs, and teens can feel cool and enjoy calling, sending pictures, and texting friends as much as they want without getting into trouble with their parents. Everyone wins.

* **Fluidity of Demand:** Customers do not stay the same; they evolve and change. Consequently, it's a mistake to view customers as existing in fixed segments or categories. In reality, customers are constantly changing and adapting through different stages in their lives and are willing to change if provided with the right opportunities. Companies can develop product/service and company loyalty by supporting customers in making these changes.

Diagnosing Context

Spheres of influence are like the ripple effect when a stone is dropped into the water, except that the ripple effects of resistance and attraction move in both directions simultaneously, from the outside in and the inside out. A *complementary innovation* strategy provides a framework with which to identify the different layers of context that influence customer behavior either toward or away from innovations. It provides guidance on how to create the right level of familiarity and comfort with change while still generating excitement at the broad socio-cultural level.

By systematically assessing the effect of the various layers of influence on the customer, it's possible to reach a much deeper understanding of *how* the customer experiences a product/service, what influences affect the quality of their experience, and what factors previous analyses failed to anticipate. With that information, one is better equipped to devise an effective strategy for identifying, developing, positioning and marketing any given product/service. For example, Dr. Robert Verganti, Professor of Management of Innovation at Politecnico di Milano in Italy, has written about how the Italian furniture consortium

Lombardy encourages people from multiple disciplines to have a community discourse about the world in which their products will be placed. He describes the community discourse in the following way: "...long before any thought is given to the form an item will eventually take, its role, identity, and meaning have been thoroughly explored. Usually the products that at long last result from this process point toward some new way of life—one that members of the community may already have started to embrace. Because the process is the sociological equivalent of basic research, most of the products it gives birth to represent a dramatic break from their predecessors."[5] In other words, a broad discussion and analysis of the socio-cultural context may identify new and emerging ways of doing things and experiencing life that the current solutions do not take into account.

Innovation is like a puzzle which needs all the pieces to be complete. Be open to looking at the world holistically.

Manager Key Takeaways

Seeking and Searching the Boundaries at the Periphery

Innovation requires companies to stretch their assumptions about *what they do, whom they serve,* and *where they should be seeking new opportunities.* Managers need to ask themselves key questions and seek answers that challenge the status quo.

- What emerging cultural and social norms will or could have an impact on the company, and what opportunities should be pursued and explored further?

- What are other emerging subcultures or countercultures for whom you can pursue with your offerings in their present form or that you can redesign and reposition?

- How well do your offerings and the positioning of your offerings fit within current values and norms?

- Have you encouraged employees (and identified particularly gifted ones) to become futurist scouts who will continuously monitor the world at large for potential opportunities related to developing cultural trends in the U.S. and abroad (kids downloading and creating movies on YouTube or interacting on FaceBook) and/or advancements in other industries that can be applied within your industry (e.g., ink jet technology as a potential drug delivery medium)?

Reduce Individual and Group Resistance Through Compatibility and Social Networks:

By thinking contextually, you cannot ignore how virtually everything is defined in large part by the context in which it exists. A different context means different rules and behaviors, which require different innovation strategies. Nothing exists in a vacuum; everything is connected. In order to create an innovation that generates more attraction than resistance – i.e., one that will fit into the context of a customer's life – companies must learn about how customers live now, then ask some hard questions:

- How does the innovation fit with the way customers are used to doing things?

- Are there incentives to make the switch to something new?

- Are the costs of switching—psychological and socio-cultural, as well as financial—worth the effort for the customer to change?

- Does the customer gain more than they lose if they switch?

- What support is available to assist in any transitions to the new solution?

Synchronicity: See the connections that are always there but only astute and attuned observers see.

To expand a perspective and avoid some cognitive biases that tend to limit a view of personal, customer, and industry experiences, here are some tips for seeing context in its fullness:

- Don't discount *any* new ideas. Establish a rule that there are no stupid ideas, and that all ideas will be heard, no matter how far-fetched they may seem initially.

- Constantly foresee the possibility of a "eureka moment" or serendipitous event by looking for unexpected, surprising results in unlikely places while also scanning the broader context.

- Make the familiar strange by flipping things around and seeing the world in an opposite light. Imagine what the familiar would look like from the view of an alien or someone new to the situation and environment.

- Constantly monitor the broader cultural trends and news. Develop a habit of asking why and how seemingly unrelated events, circumstances, or developments can be relevant to your business problem. Innovation and creativity requires people to "absorb and read the world" like an early warning system, looking for "hotspots" and tipping points in the culture that are ripe to take-off and "cold" spots that are overdue for change. As Ogle recommends, "Try to see the world not as you wish it to be, but as it is... You'll always be in some box, so instead of rebelling against it, map the major hubs [culture] dominating it. In general, look at the space around you and figure out how to make it think for you."[6] Work at putting the puzzle together.

- Be patient because changes happen slowly over time. It is important to keep track of emerging cultural trends and to see as the story unfolds; however, be aware that the story almost always takes longer than hoped for or expected.

- Trying to get one's mind around all of the possible socio-cultural influences on people and products at any given point in time is a daunting task. Be careful not to focus on too many factors at once. The mind can only focus on a limited number of factors at a time, and therefore it is best to focus on 5-7 key factors in order to keep track of them over time. If something of new relevance and interest emerges, then replace one of the least relevant current factors so the tracking process can remain manageable. Do not fall into the cognitive bias, known as the information bias, where people believe that acquiring more information will lead to a better decision when, in fact, the additional information will not affect the outcome because the information is not relevant. The challenge is to avoid the trap of analysis paralysis.

- Continually refresh the picture of the situation as it relates to the innovation since the world is always in flux. Any assessment is really a momentary snapshot of a dynamic and ever-changing set of factors, and should be treated as such.

- Waiting on innovations is sometimes the best option. In some cases, the smart thing to do is hold off the introduction of an innovation because the contextual factors do not align and the timing isn't quite right. If too many factors are currently out of sync, it is important to determine what needs to occur before the concept will fly.

- Read broadly to look for emerging trends. Besides the newspaper and television/radio news programs, read from sources that encourage broad thinking: www.trend-watching.com, *Wired, Business Week, The Economist,* http://www.sciencenews.org, *www.KurzweilAI.net, The World Futurist Society (www.wfs.org), www.faithpopcorn.com, Coastal Living, Harvard Business Review, Forbes, Fortune, Newsweek, Real Simple, Popular Mechanics* – no source is too far a field.

- Looking broadly makes it easier to detect emerging competitors before it is too late to respond. Market leaders aren't always unseated by traditional competitors; they are often displaced by an emerging competitor that has been circling for some time on the periphery. Such peripheral competition has a nasty way of sneaking up on companies. All too often, companies and industries—especially established ones—begin to view their solutions as inherently superior, and to unwittingly believe that their way is the only way to meet customer's needs. It never is, and it's best not to learn that bitter lesson the hard way.

- Probably one of the most important manager takeaways is accepting that it is impossible to predict the future, and that the willingness to take chances at the risk of being wrong is indicative of an innovative mindset. Managers need to foster an environment within which it is okay to be wrong but not to be stupid--intelligent risk-taking vs. reckless stupidity. Use methods such as scenario planning and foresighting. Read Peter Schwartz's book *The Art of the Long View: Planning for the Future in an Uncertain World* and the Peter Bishop and Andy Hines book, *Thinking about the Future: Guidelines for Strategic Foresight,* to guide you through the process of identifying the critical contextual factors and assumptions that influence your thinking about potential futures.[7, 8]

Chapter 6

Customer Needs—Why Do Products and Services Exist in the First Place?

"Modern man lives under the illusion that he knows what he wants, while he actually wants what he is supposed to want."

~Erich Fromm, *Escape from Freedom* (1941)

James Lipton said of actors: "All of us...eventually arrive at the same place, which is the heart, mind, and soul of the audience. That's where we're all going..."[1] Companies are not unlike actors in that all of their actions need to capture the heart, mind, and soul of the customer as their needs are met. According to the Merriam-Webster dictionary, a *need* is "a lack of something requisite, desirable, or useful; a physiological or psychological requirement for the well-being of an organism," or "anything that is necessary but lacking." For our purposes, we define the act of "meeting a need," as what happens when someone accomplishes a goal and/or satisfies a desire through their customer experience with an offering.

Every offering exists and is intended to fill some sort of need or desire, so it stands to reason that knowledge of the need a customer is trying to address is something with which a company ought to be familiar. Unfortunately, this is not always the case. All too often, companies are so wrapped up in their products, services, and processes from their own perspective that they forget about the crucial psychology of their customers – the basic reasons why customers choose their offerings or not.

Now our focus is on understanding what makes customers tick through the crucial interaction between offerings and the customer. Putting the customer first isn't just a slogan or talking point, rather it's a management philosophy that affects all parts of the organization and, if done correctly, can – and should – transform the way almost everything in a company is done.

Below is a representation of an integrated framework for innovation based on the work of Gibson and Maslow.[2, 3, 4] The dif-

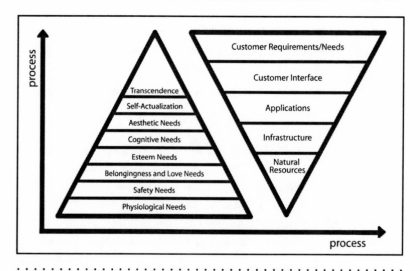

Figure 6.1

ference between this view and a more traditional view is that this view takes the environmental structure into account, as well as the needs of the customer and the interaction between them.

This framework depicts a hierarchy of customer needs on the left side of the graphic, the immediate product/service environment on the right, and the all-important processes that govern their interaction enveloping them both.

The upright pyramid, based on Maslow's "hierarchy of needs," represents the types of needs customers actively try to fulfill. Abraham Maslow is best known for this model of human motivation, which depicts people's most essential needs from basic requirements such as thirst and hunger, to reaching their full potential and helping others realize their potential. *Maslow's hierarchy is useful for innovators because it identifies types of needs that all human beings are wired to fulfill.*

The inverted pyramid to the right of the customer-needs pyramid partitions the product/service environment into the various layers of potential barriers to acceptance and adoption of the product/service. (We focus attention on the immediate product/service environment in Chapter 7) As discussed earlier, James Gibson argued that in order to understand something – an animal, person, product, or event – it is necessary to understand the environment, or context, in which it exists or takes place. As Gibson said, "It's not what is inside the head that is important; it's what the head is inside of." *The core premise is that acceptance and adoption is significantly driven by the offering's overall design from top to bottom of the product/service environment pyramid.*

New offerings provide opportunities that weren't possible before. These new opportunities, called affordances by Gibson, don't do anything by themselves, however -- they need an actor to engage with them. The actor – i.e., the consumer – brings their own experience, needs, and preferences to any given set of affordances in an environment, and must take advantage of the information and possibilities to meet his/her need. Thus, the quality of the design of the customer's experience to a large extent determines how the offering communicates its benefits and its "friendliness" to a variety of customers; good design speaks to a wide range of customers and captures each of them based on what they need. This approach puts the company in greater control of its own destiny because they can anticipate and/or make adjustments to the layers of the product/service environment pyramid.

Finally, the framework depicts the customer needs and product/service pyramids surrounded by the "process" (or processes) that guide the relationship between the customer and the product/service as the customer attempts to achieve a goal or desired experience. In the act of innovation, every interaction between a customer and an offering should be viewed as part of a process – a continuing sequence of activities – whose ultimate goal is the fulfillment of customer needs. This puts the customer (rather than the company) at the center of the innovation process, and all of the links in the decision chain, leading up to a marketable innovation, will ideally pass through the prism of the customer. Michael Gates Gill described his achievement of a superior rating from a "secret customer" in process terms in his book *How Starbucks Saved My Life.*[5] "The key criteria are:

- Do you make eye contact?

- Do you greet the guest?

- Do you thank the guest?

- Do you initiate conversation?

- Do you recognize a guest by the drink they typically order or name?"

The customer experience is all the little details of process. One misstep in the interaction and the customer experience can fall apart. We will now focus on the customer needs side of the interaction equation and its role in innovation.

Focus on the Customer Needs

The psychology of human behavior holds an important key to making innovation success happen. If companies understand what customers bring to situations, they will be better equipped to understand what customers get out of offerings and why they respond the way they do. Maslow's theory provides an informative and insightful way of looking at customer needs and understanding what motivates people.

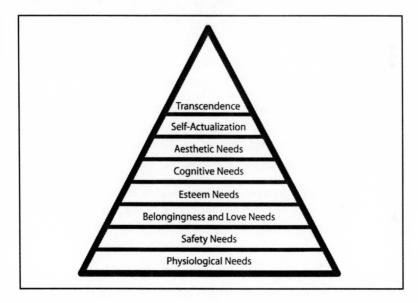

Figure 6.2

Maslow's needs hierarchy includes:

- **Physiological needs** such as food, water, sleep, and sex. The axiom, "It's difficult to philosophize on an empty stomach" comes to mind here. Have you ever shopped for groceries when you were hungry?

- **Safety/Security:** Protection from harm must be assured before a person can pursue other goals. Home and family are an important source of security, as are cultural norms and laws.

- **Belongingness and Love:** Social needs such as affiliation, acceptance from others, love and a sense of community or belonging. Camaraderie and companionship are necessary ingredients of happiness.

- **Esteem:** People seek attention, approval, recognition, and respect from others. They strive to be seen as competent and needed by others. At its highest level, this desire includes the need for power and the admiration to lift one's feelings of self-worth. Products that symbolize a certain level of social prestige or distinction are important. The Rolex watches, the Mercedes Benz, the Armani suit – all are purchased in no small part to fill the buyer's need for recognition and respect.

- **Cognitive** needs are associated with the desire to know, understand and explore the world, curiosity and motivation to understand and find answers to questions through inquiry and knowledge.

- **Aesthetic** needs reflect the desire to find beauty, symmetry, and order in our lives and in the world around us. Superior design is often reflected in its ability to speak to customers' desire for fulfilling their aesthetic needs.

- **Self-Actualization** and/or self-fulfillment needs are associated with achieving one's potential as a human being; achieving one's goals in life, whether through travel, art, entrepreneurship, self-sacrifice, spiritual devotion, etc.

- **Transcendence** is the need and desire to connect with something beyond one's self and/or to help others achieve self-actualization as well. People can try to help others reach their potential and self-fulfillment once they no longer have to focus on meeting their own needs. It will be interesting to see how the market for "self-actualization" and "transcendence" develops further as record numbers of baby boomers retire and can focus more of their attention on the meaning of their lives, individually and collectively.

Maslow saw need fulfillment as a hierarchical ladder, which people traverse one step at a time from the bottom of the pyramid (basic physiological needs) to the top (self actualization and transcendence). More recently, his work has been viewed as too rigid in its presumption that the hierarchy of needs has to be traversed in a specific order. Although not one hundred percent foolproof and accurate, Maslow provided a useful guide for thinking about what motivates and shapes customers' needs. In particular, customers are willing to make choices and trade-offs about what will meet their needs. With increased affluence in the United States and many other parts of the world, people are seeking personal fulfillment, purpose, and meaning beyond basic needs. In their 2003 book, *Trading Up: The New American Luxury*, Michael Silverstein and Neil Fiske point out that customers are willing to pay a premium for goods that meet particular needs that suit their desires.[6] In essence, different people derive fulfillment and satisfaction from different things and are willing to make trade-offs to acquire them. For example, someone may really like to play golf and is willing to make compromises in other parts of their life so that they can afford expensive golf clubs and green's fees, while another person may compromise in order to collect fine wines or invest in real estate.

Silverstein and Friske identify different types of customers and the areas they are willing to trade-up to:

- **Taking care of me products/services** that help ease stress, reward accomplishments and provide solace (bedding, personal care, and spas);

- **Connecting products/services** that help people build, maintain and enrich their relationships with significant people in their immediate environment (family, friends, colleagues, significant others). Dining out, cruises, cell-phone services, etc.

- **Questing** products/services that give customers the opportunity to try new experiences, learn about ideas and cultures, and broaden their perspective (e.g., travel, wines, books);

- **Individual style** products/services that support consumers in their desire to express themselves and associate themselves with brands (e.g., cars, watches, clothes).

Another example of how fulfilling one's needs has changed is an emerging segment of mothers who some call "yoga mamas." These women see motherhood as a personal statement and a part of fulfilling their own needs. According to Linda Murray, editor of www.babycenter.com, these middle- and upper-income mothers are "extending their lifestyle to their babies."[7] They are focused on being active, fit, and healthy during pregnancy, and are re-defining motherhood as a means of self-fulfillment. Regardless of income, these college-educated mothers are spending significant resources on stylish, brand name items that they believe will give their children an edge in terms of health and well being, both physically and psychologically. When it comes to supporting their children's development and health, no expense is spared. Only the most stylish, highest-quality merchandise will do —from $700 strollers, to $11.50 baby cream, to $150 diaper bags, to $70 play mats. The yoga mamas' desire to provide the best for their children is influencing the entire baby products industry, as well as the larger parenting culture. This is a trend to track.

Clearly, there are many people who are trying to fulfill needs that go beyond the means-to-an-end basic needs. We don't just buy offerings to get things done or accomplish a task; we also want to be entertained and pampered, we want beautiful things, we want to be connected to others, we want to have meaning and purpose in life, and we want to feel important, needed, or affluent. How the product/service makes a customer feel and whether it provides a way for the customer to express his or her values, feelings, and personality is as critical as its functionality. The cars we drive, the clothes and accessories we wear, and even the consumer electronics we use go beyond the functional and reflects who we are or how we want to be perceived.

Taking it even a step further, customers are finding new ways of fulfilling their needs through emerging social mediums such as blogs, message boards, podcasts, wikis, vlogs, YouTube, Facebook, MySpace, and Second Life. In Second Life, subscribers can create a virtual life from scratch. The experience includes creating an online graphic persona or avatar, having online friends and relationships, roaming around virtual landscapes and cityscapes, even building virtual homes and businesses. Second Life allows subscribers to fulfill their needs through a virtual existence that unshackles them from the constraints of their real lives in an anonymous fashion. Second Life is a great example of the 4P's of innovation in action, particularly from a paradigm perspective. In essence, the products and services and processes (*products* and *processes*) are all occurring in a virtual environment (*paradigm*) and the challenge for companies is to *position* this virtual offering to the right set of customers who are willing to pay real money for the experience.

Whose needs are we trying to fulfill?

It may seem simplistic, but one of the key challenges for companies is to figure out whom to speak with when trying to identify the next product/service opportunity. At first blush this may seem painfully obvious, but it really isn't, because companies often grab the first customer who will talk to them. Unfortunately, the term *customer* can be used just as imprecisely as the term *market*, and create just as much confusion. Companies are often lazy about defining who the customer really is; for example, is it the actual user, the purchase decision-maker, or both? In many cases, the purchase decision-maker and the actual user are the same, but not always. It is especially important to separate the roles when the purchaser and user are different.

For example, in commercial aviation, Boeing and Airbus serve the needs of commercial airlines (purchase decision-maker) while at the same time they are trying to meet the needs of the actual end users, a group that includes pilots, flight attendants, mechanics, and, of course, passengers. In the home-building industry, manufacturers of air conditioning and temperature control systems, such as Honeywell, serve builders and distributors who may want a feature/functionality-rich product such as a thermostat that is easy to install, low in price (high profit margin), and requires little service. A homeowner, on the other hand, may want a system with a few key features that is easy to operate on a daily basis and backed by exceptional service.

When talking about the end user it is important to consider the degree of interaction that the customer has with the offering. In many cases, there is a primary user who spends a significant amount of time interacting with the offering. Secondary users interact with the offering less frequently and may never use the primary functionality but benefit from the output of the offering. For example, a secondary user may receive a report or analysis that is generated from a product that allows him/her to get their job done.

When pursuing innovation, one of the biggest mistakes companies can make is to miss the opportunity of attracting "new customers." Christensen and Raynor (2003) and Kim and Mauborgne (2005) identified different reasons why people are *not* customers, based on their behavior, their general feelings toward the product/service, and their awareness of the product/ service.[8,9] The goal is to recognize and understand where and what will result in resistance to the offering.

- **Low End Market Customers** (Price at the expense of features and performance): Price drives decision-making as long as their needs are met at an acceptable level; they desire the basics without all the bells and whistles. Is it the case that the current offerings are so feature and performance rich for status quo customers that these potential customers are an untapped opportunity? Consider other ways of attracting customers besides focusing on price alone. Perhaps, price is the easy way out, but not the best approach for long-term profitability. What about stripping away functionality (and thus reducing price) while at the same time providing a highly usable and pleasant interaction and overall experience?

- **First-Tier Non-Customers** (*soon-to-b*e): Customers who use the product/service on a limited basis and are eagerly seeking an alternative, superior solution. Once they find an alternative, they will switch to it instantly. The challenge is to understand why they do not perceive the current offering as the long-term solution. Put a prototype into the hands of customers very early in the design process. It opens the eyes of the user to the possibilities. It provides an opportunity to work the kinks out early--before the offering is even in the market as well.

- **Second-Tier Non-Customers** or new market disruption, in Christensen's terminology (*refusing*): These are customers who will not or cannot use the current solution. This type of non-customer will not use the product/service because it is either unacceptable or too expensive. Customers refuse to use the current solution because of a variety of barriers such as a lack of skills or money. Can the user experience be improved to make it more accessible by making it more convenient to access and/or easier to use? Or can a superior service experience be developed that attracts people to hire out the activity?

- **Third-Tier Non-Customers** (*unexplored*): Customers who have been assumed to reside in a different industry and have therefore not been thought of as potential customers. Most companies assume that since someone else is meeting the needs of these customers, why bother with them? But what if you can provide an alternative product/service that is superior to what these customers are currently using? Assuming that customers are interested in having their needs met, why should it matter where the solution comes from?

The first three types of non-customers have experience with the offering but choose not to accept and adopt it. In all cases, a better customer experience can reduce resistance by making the offering easier to use and accessible. The fourth type of non-customer is the most interesting in that customer needs can be met in highly differentiated ways by providing a newer solution than anything currently available. If done right, it can create a lot of excitement because it goes against the status quo.

Clearly defining which customers the company is targeting is critical and requires the company to dig a little deeper. Ask: Whose needs are we trying to meet? How do the needs of the various *customers* in a value chain differ? Do some customers' needs conflict with those of others? For whom do we optimize? Can we optimize for everyone? We need to distinguish between and consider all customers in the design and development process so that we are at least making trade-offs explicitly and exhaustively. Consider the different ways in which the concept of a *customer* can be defined from the standpoint of what role they play in the purchase, usage, and interaction process with a product or service.

Capturing and sorting through customer needs

A key challenge for companies is to figure out where to focus their attention in terms of satisfying customer needs that are not being met. Unmet needs are, of course, what innovations try to address. The challenge is to identify those unmet needs and address them with innovations that not only serve their intended function, but also excite and delight customers enough to turn them into product evangelists. Customers are generally better at describing what they *don't* want than articulating what they do want. In addition, they are good at identifying possible improvements to current solutions and current state of affairs, but not at coming up with entirely new ideas themselves. An apt quote that illustrates this point is from Henry Ford regarding the automobile: "If I'd asked my customers what they wanted, they'd have said a faster horse." Because this is the most common type of information that customers provide, it's also what tends to drive product design and marketing. To innovate, companies need to go beyond what customers say and answer a few key questions in depth:

- What do they need?

- Why do they need it?

- What is stopping them from committing to a particular solution?

- What needs to be there for them to know that they have met their needs?

There are usually a number of unspoken or unarticulated needs that customers never mention. There are at least three reasons why customers do not bring up certain needs. First, they often do not communicate what they expect because they assume it is provided. For example, a physician assumes that a medical device is safe and ready for implant and will provide physiological benefits for the patient. These are the expected qualities of a reputable medical device, so it wouldn't occur to the physician to doubt them.

A second reason that customers leave some things unsaid is that they have trouble imagining what they have not yet experienced or do not know. Someone who is not a medical technician would be unlikely to know what sort of engineering modifications might be necessary to improve the performance of a pacemaker. Their knowledge and experience limits their imagination, which limits the scope of advice they can credibly offer.

A third reason is that customers are sometimes not even

aware of what they need or want, or why they need or want it. In such cases, the term *unarticulated needs* is a misnomer. A better term would be *unrecognized needs* because, by the time most people are able to articulate their need the opportunity to build an innovation around it has already passed. Furthermore, verbal feedback is incomplete and sometimes inaccurate because people are not particularly good judges of their own motives and behavior. For example, people sometimes say what they think another person wants to hear, withhold information for fear of looking stupid, or not realize that their actions are a result of stress. People also often omit many details or, conversely, embellish them.

In any case, as noted earlier, companies need to go beyond simply asking customers what they need and taking their verbal feedback at face value, because it is inherently filtered, incomplete, and sometimes inaccurate and biased. In addition, their feedback focuses on the status quo and thus will only provide information that yields incremental improvements. This means that companies need to go beyond the typical focus groups, interviews, and surveys. In pursuit of understanding customer needs, wants, and desires, it is critical to assess needs in the context of the spheres of influence (Chapter 5) to appreciate how customer needs evolve in their environment. Companies need to be astute observers of customers in their natural environment to identify unarticulated, unrecognized needs, wants, and desires that will spark more radical innovation.

Once customer needs have been identified, they shouldn't just be *told* about an idea, they should be allowed to interact and experiment with concepts and prototype customer experience designs, particularly when the needs were unrecognized and the concept is new. People are better at providing feedback with a concept they can interact with and experience through their senses. This allows them to discover the benefits and to compare the effectiveness either positively or negatively against their current solution. Furthermore, customer segmentation based on actual experience provides unique insight into the different benefits that customers perceive. The value of this information cannot be overstated because it is based on concrete real experience with the actual concept (e.g., real impressions and feelings about the offering) rather than a one-sided impression that is filled with biases based on personality tendencies and motivations. Allowing customers to experience the concept breaks down their inherent resistance to change, and also provides insights into the dynamics of resistance that a company might encounter when the final product/service is released. Companies can identify unique customer segments based on experience with the concept that customers would not have otherwise mentioned.

Knowledge is power . . . to innovate

A *complementary innovation* strategy focuses on customer needs within the social and physical environment. Companies often go wrong because they have not focused on the basics such as clearly identifying *who* are the customers, *what* are their needs, *why* are they seeking to fulfill the needs, and *how* are those needs currently being satisfied. Without this knowledge companies mistakenly move forward with inadequate or mistaken assumptions and knowledge that lead to solutions that customers don't need or want.

Manager Key Takeaways

Customer needs emerge out the relationship between the customer, the offering, and the broader environmental context. With this deeper understanding of what motivates customers as they seek out different products and services, companies can develop, design and market innovations more effectively. Some key questions managers need to ask themselves are:

- Have we really identified who we need to understand and why (e.g., user, purchaser)?

- Do we understand what motivates the customer to accept or reject an offering?

- Do we have a way of identifying recognized and unrecognized customer needs?

- Have we put in place a process and methods for developing and evaluating concepts with customers to get robust feedback on whether the concepts hit the mark in terms of meeting customer needs and wants?

- What resources are available to provide the basic needs of customers? In general, if someone is living in a place where food and water are scarce, disease is rampant, and medical help and sanitation are nonexistent, meeting basic needs for safety and security is likely to be a higher priority than worrying about self-actualization and transcendence.

- What socio-cultural constraints or supports are present that influence customers' needs? Consider movements such as Slow Food (www.slowfood.com), which encourages people to live a particular type of life: "Slow Food is a non-profit, eco-gastronomic member-supported organization that was founded in 1989 to counteract fast food and fast life, the disappearance of local food traditions and people's dwindling interest in the food they eat, where it comes from, how it tastes, and how our food choices affect the rest of the world."

- Have any events influenced people? After 9/11, many questioned the meaning and purpose of their lives.

- Can you see how different people are motivated and how they process information differently?

- Are there any current circumstances in the lives of customers that may influence their behavior?

- Are there ways in which your offering can be recommended to the customer right at the moment when they need it? A start-up called BlueTie is exploring an advertising concept called "featuretisements" that presents a very specific advertisement based on the content of a user's e-mail, calendar, or messages on social networking sites. For example, if a user types in information about a trip to Minneapolis into their calendar, a "featuretisement" would be generated regarding detailed flight schedules for that day. The value of a service like this is that it puts advertisement in context based on the current needs of the potential customer. This approach goes beyond the traditional method of blasting the advertising message out into the ether in hopes of capturing the attention and interest of potential targeted customers. As BlueTie founder David Koretz says: "You have to see intent [of the user], and then not annoy the hell out of people." He goes on to say: "If you make advertisement feel like features, people will use it."[10] How can you anticipate the needs of potential customers and seamlessly provide your offering to them without them feeling bothered?

- Are you looking in emerging contexts such as virtual social networking communities to identify new ways in which customers are fulfilling their needs? By enlisting the right people to help us, we are essentially making them co-creators of the offering. They are the end-users, after all, so it makes sense to tap into their knowledge *before* the final product is released, rather than hearing about your mistakes afterwards through customer complaints.

Chapter 7

The Structure of Innovation: Communication between the Environment, the Product, and the Customer

"Nothing is rich but the inexhaustible wealth of nature. She shows us only surfaces, but she is a million fathoms deep."

~Ralph Waldo Emerson

Superior design of customer experiences is a requirement for success, particularly when it comes to innovation. Product design that makes it easy to use while exuding beauty and style clearly attracts customers. People recognize it when they see it; the challenge is to figure out how to regularly hit the mark in a predictable manner rather than it being an infrequent, serendipitous event.

The effectiveness and success of an offering has just as

much to do with the environment in which that product/service is used as it does with the individual customer. Recall that psychologist James Gibson's theory of "affordances" includes the idea that objects in the environment communicates certain qualities about their usefulness to the people observing them.[1,2] An example of how affordances work is illustrated in the 1980 movie *The Gods Must Be Crazy*, in which the Sho people of the Kalahari are introduced to a Coke bottle and believe it is a gift from the gods. When the Sho people encounter the Coke bottle, it comes to them completely context-free. They don't know what it is, what it's for, or where it came from, so they discover things to do with it. They find many different uses for the bottle, such as a game piece, musical instrument, rolling pin, and finally a weapon. The story of the Post-It Note® has some similarities in that market testing yielded mixed results and the product was nearly killed many times.[3] However, once customers tried it in Boise, Idaho, in 1978, ninety percent of them said they would buy it. In fact, when the product was introduced in eleven western states, customers started shipping it to co-workers in areas where it was unavailable. Once it was put into the hands of people, they found numerous uses for it. Now the Post-it Note® is everywhere and has turned into hundreds of products with different uses.

Affordances are a part of our daily lives, whether we know it or not. The trick is to create a harmonious marriage between the environment, the customer, and the product so that this communication happens as spontaneously and naturally as possible. Ideally, this is the state of mind all innovations should attempt to inspire.

Good designers use their understanding of the overall environmental context to *design in* the interactions and affordances that will lead to the customer experience they're trying to provide. If you create an offering that works better than customers expect, they will be both satisfied *and* delighted. If you can provide them something that *amazes* them, they will be more than delighted – they will be eager to tell everyone they know about their new discovery. A Philips advertisement that captures the essence of good design states: "Simplicity is technology that fits seamlessly into your life." In design circles, it is considered a hallmark of elegant design if an object can communicate to a person how it is supposed to be used – that is, if the secrets of operating it are implied in the design. If a person can just pick something up and start using it – it represents an ideal marriage of product design and customer need. Achieving this sort of idiot-proof ease of use is not simple, as anyone who has tried to learn all the intricacies of their television remote control can tell you.

If companies embrace the assumption that, as Gibson says, the environment is structured and meaningful, it can change their perspective and help them design superior products and services. If one assumes that the environment can significantly influence customer behavior, then a company can create many opportunities to directly observe or manipulate various environmental factors and obtain meaningful data with which to work. Practically speaking, this is far more constructive than sitting around with a bunch of colleagues trying to figure out what is going on in a customer's head – or worse, trying to separate what a customer *says* they are thinking from what they are *really* thinking.

The rest of this chapter offers a framework for understanding the *structure* of the product/service environment so that offerings can be deliberately designed to satisfy the customer. By the end of the chapter, it will be clear how to use this framework to achieve results intentionally rather than by accident. The goal is to move beyond price and basic quality as the basis of competitive advantage and create a customer experience that is in high demand and commands premium prices. Move from the basics, which are already assumed to be there by the customer (me-to products/services), to *delighting* the customer and pulling away from the competition. Products and services should look sharp, function intuitively and wake some sort of positive emotional response for the consumer. As noted in the previous chapter, our model for the customer environment looks like this:

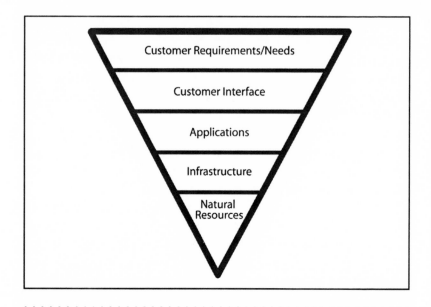

Figure 7.1

Natural Resources (both physical and social)

Natural resources serve as the foundation and fuel for innovation by providing the basic building blocks and elements that are transformed into innovations. They include raw materials such as coal, water, land, oil, and minerals, as well as physical forces and constraints, including the laws of nature. Let's extend the above definition of natural resources to include living things such as plants, animals, and our fellow human beings. Humans have used natural resources in extraordinary ways over the course of history. We have learned how to surmount many of the constraints of the physical world and harness the laws of physics and chemistry to create a multitude of solutions that did not exist before. Through an understanding of nature's basic building blocks, we have continually been able to extend their reach in the physical world and use them to meet our physical, social, and emotional needs.

Throughout history, close observation of nature has stimulated people's imagination and provided the building blocks and analogs and metaphors for new ideas; consider the many ideas of Leonardo da Vinci. Today, there are those that believe the study of nature can still be the basis of innovation through imitation; it is called biomimicry (from bios, meaning life, and mimesis, meaning to imitate). Examples include bat-inspired walking canes to abalone-inspired ceramic materials to termite-inspired air conditioners (www.biomimicry.net/casestudiesB. htm). Perhaps, taking a step back and communing with nature is not a bad idea in our chaotic and hectic existence.

Infrastructure

Infrastructure is built on natural resources and, as the word implies, it provides the "structure" upon which human activities rely. It is human beings applying their know-how and creativity to extend the usefulness of the natural resources available in the world. Taking what is available, and extending its uses, provides greater utility and flexibility.

Infrastructure can take various forms. It can be built upon physical resources, such as the infrastructure for transportation and communication systems, water and power lines, as well as public institutions such as schools, post offices, and prisons. Other types of infrastructure include the genetic modification of plants and animals, synthesis of drugs, and even plastic surgery are examples of how we have altered living things for our use. Nanotechnology is the ability to transform matter at the molecular level to create healthcare products such as implantable medical devices and nano-drug agents, as well as nano-electronics for chips, memory, and displays.

Infrastructure that can serve as a platform or underlying foundation for creating various applications provides unique value that companies can exploit for long-term sustainability. For example, in the pharmaceutical industry, certain drug families ("platforms") are used to address multiple diseases and ailments. Likewise, in the automotive industry, manufacturers use many of the same components or modules in different vehicles, using the frame of a truck, say, and building a mini-van around it.

Infrastructure is a necessary foundation for any innovation or process. The challenge for companies is that the risk and reward pay-off of investing in infrastructure can be very high. Over the past twenty years, numerous companies have chewed through billions of investment dollars in the build-out of the broadband infrastructure that now serves the United States. The companies involved in developing this broadband infrastructure mistakenly took the "if you build it, they will come" approach, but were unable to communicate and deliver the promised benefits (e.g., movies-on-demand, high-speed Internet, Internet phones, security systems). These companies fell into Moore's chasm and experienced numerous funding shortages before they could deliver the promised applications that would eventually create the tornado of demand powerful enough to drive them up the adoption curve. The fruits of all their labor are paying off now that applications are finally emerging and broadband penetration is increasing. Unfortunately, many of the companies that took the risk to build this broadband infrastructure went bankrupt along the way.

Applications

Remember, customers are always actively seeking to meet their needs and improve the quality of their lives. If the current solutions do not meet their needs, they will seek out other solutions. Likewise, if the new solutions offered are no better than the old ones, people will not feel compelled to switch or change. Customers are practical, and they want things to work, particularly in the realm of technology. According to Steve Jobs, "We live in an era where more and more of our activities depend on technology. We take our photos without film and have to do something with them to make them usable. We get our music over the Internet and carry it around in digital music players. It's in your automobile and your kitchen."[4]

Try replacing Jobs' use of the term *technology* with the term *application*. The creations that directly benefit customers are applications. One definition for *application* is "a method of putting something to a special use or purpose." We define an application as human knowledge that has been discovered or conceived and formed into a useful configuration that meets customer needs. This includes both products and services, because products provide "tools," and services provide knowledge of how to engage in an activity more effectively. It's fulfilling needs, whether it's related to basic physical or physiological well being and safety, or to social companionship and achieving one's wildest dreams.

Customer Interface

The customer "interface" is the point of interaction or communication between the customer and the product/service. Communication is the key factor here. The challenge for companies is to define an interaction in such a way that it fits how the customer thinks. Otherwise, it's like two people speaking different languages. Superior interaction design requires an understanding of the goals the user is trying to achieve, and determining what needs to be communicated between the product and the user for a successful interaction to happen. A helpful definition of an interaction is the balance between the *task,* the *user,* and the *product* to achieve a particular *purpose.* Too often, companies want to jump to specific design and visualization solutions that include widgets, knobs, or shapes, without understanding the aspects of interaction or communication they are really trying to address.

The customer interface involves what we call *customer* performance rather than *technical* performance. Often when companies talk about performance, they focus on the technology. How fast is the processor? How many calculations can be done in a second? How much data can be transferred over that cable? Customer performance, on the other hand, focuses on how the solution is performing *for the customer.* Does it make their life easier? Are the benefits obvious? Is the technology serving a purpose beyond its improved specifications? Thinking about *customer performance* requires thinking about the interaction between the customer and the product/service from a social rather than a technical viewpoint. The best measure of performance is the degree to which customers can accomplish their goals in a satisfactory and pleasing manner. For example, if a processor on an electronic device can execute a command in a matter of milliseconds, but the user interaction is so confusing that it takes the user twenty minutes to figure out what to do, what's the point of the technical performance? The interaction is a failure, and you can bet the customer will not be happy. *Overall* performance is a combination of both the system and the customer. Thus, minimum technical performance requirements must be met for the interaction to be successful. If the technical performance cannot keep up with the user, the overall interaction will fail.

Expanding Opportunities

Customers see their overall experiences on a continuum from positive and satisfying, to negative and disappointing. The framework we have presented provides a way to systematically view the product/service environment to more easily strengthen the customer relationship, while minimizing the effort necessary on the company's part to deliver value to the customer. The product/service pyramid is wider at the top because the number of solution options increases from the bottom of the pyramid as it moves to the top. One example of this widening is the fact that the number of platforms for automobiles is fairly small, while the number of automobile types that customers perceive as different and unique is much larger.

Mark Twain observed: "There is no such thing as new idea...We simply take a lot of old ideas and put them into a sort of mental kaleidoscope. We give them a turn and they make new and curious combinations. We keep on turning and making new combinations indefinitely; but they are the same old pieces of colored glass that have been in use through all the ages."

Our *complementary innovation* approach challenges companies to see customer needs and solutions as having two different kinds of relationships: many-to-one, and one-to-many. The product/service environment is depicted as an inverted pyramid to represent the fact that the world provides *many solutions to one need* and that *one solution can serve many needs*, depending on the customer. A product/service can be used in multiple ways in the hands of different customers, who bring different needs and backgrounds to different situations. A visit to the web site www.ducttapeguys.com provides an object lesson in this kind of thinking. The Duct Tape Guys have created an entire industry out of a humble roll of duct tape, raising it from an occasionally useful product to a cultural icon of do-it-yourself ingenuity. On their site are tips for using duct tape (some practical, most ridiculous), and they sell t-shirts, mugs, lunch boxes, and everything else you can think of – all because they had the ingenuity to apply a sense of humor to a simple roll of tape.

Alternatively, multiple solutions may fulfill a very specific need, depending on the customer. For example, how many ways are there to communicate with others? You can call on the phone, e-mail, write a traditional letter, instant message, interact via Webcam, hold a videoconference or shout across the room. Depending on individual circumstances, individuals will select the solution that best suits their needs. Jeff Hawkin understood what his Palm Pilot was competing against: "I realized that my competition was paper, not computers." Likewise, your future competition may not be obvious right now, and the solution for remaining competitive may not be obvious, either. Whatever the situation, however, there are likely to be more possible solutions than the players in any given market may realize.

In order to broaden the palette of possibilities a company can offer to customers, ask: *What* else can this product/services be used for? *Where* else can it be used? Employing this principle of many-to-one and one-to-many has two benefits for companies: first, it reminds us to look beyond the current solutions and competitors to avoid being surprised, and second, it encourages us to find new markets and customers.

Resources and infrastructure are necessary for a company to operate, of course, but it is from the upper layers of the pyramid that resources and infrastructure can be most effectively leveraged. The applications and customer interface layers are where multiple benefits, or affordances, can be created, because these layers are the ones that most directly touch the customer. This is where the "experience" of a company's products/services starts making an important difference. Companies need to migrate up the product/service pyramid to sustain growth. Over time, infrastructure companies either have to find multiple uses for their infrastructure or move up the pyramid to applications and services to maintain revenues. A company can remain successful for a long time by focusing on infrastructure if it is agile at identifying new markets where its technology can be utilized. Texas Instruments pursued this strategy brilliantly. TI used its expertise in microchip design to create a computer chip architecture flexible enough to support a wide range of next-generation digital applications such as mobile phones, broadband modems, digital cameras, MP3 players, projectors, and flat-screen televisions, along with several wireless technologies and medical devices.[5] From a customer standpoint, the technology is invisible; customers only care about the benefits that the infrastructure (the chip) provides. Meanwhile, Texas Instruments is identifying multiple uses for its platform technologies in various application domains. The greater challenge comes later as the technology infrastructure matures in various market segments and the competition drives down prices in those segments.

In contrast to Texas Instruments' approach, many companies have tried to grow by migrating up from the infrastructure to the application layer of the pyramid. Intel and Cisco are two examples of companies moving up the product/service pyramid to direct interaction with the customer. Intel has been highly successful in providing the microprocessor or *brain* of most personal computers in the world, now including the Apple Mac. For many years, Intel focused on being part of the infrastructure of personal computing and created a powerful brand image around its slogan *Intel Inside™*. Recently, the company changed its marketing campaign and brand image based on a new slogan: *Intel. Leap Ahead™*. According to Intel's marketing literature, "Leap ahead declares who we are and where we are going... In the end, it's not just about making technology faster, smarter, and cheaper—it's about using that technology to make life better, richer, and more convenient for everyone it touches."[6] It is no surprise that Intel has made a major strategic investment in the healthcare industry. The company's strategy is to start finding ways to bring value directly to the customer rather than simply providing the supporting infrastructure for profitable computer-based products.

Similarly, Cisco has been moving up the product/service pyramid as well. Besides services, they are now much closer to the consumer through home networking (Linksys) and set-top boxes and digital video recorders (Scientific Atlanta) that create a convergence of video, voice, and data. The company revamped its logo to shift the emphasis away from Cisco's products per se, to *how these products connect people* through what they are calling the "Human Network."[7] Interestingly, Cisco, like Intel, has a strategic emphasis on the healthcare industry. Both companies are evolving from being primarily behind-the-scenes infrastructure companies to providing applications and services that touch the customer directly.

Developing a Closer Relationship with the Customer for Mutual Benefit

The quality of the customer's experience with a product or service is going to determine its success. Steve Jobs summed up Apple's formula for success this way: "Apple's core strength is to bring very high technology to mere mortals in a way that surprises and delights them and they can figure out how to use."[8] Infrastructure may enable innovation, but it can also be a major barrier to the adoption of innovation. Companies need to make sure that their products/services are compatible with the current infrastructure while still providing unique value, differentiation, reduced switching costs and ease-of-use for the customer. For example, Gerard Kleisterlee, CEO of Philips Electronics, believes that if leading companies like Apple and Sony stopped focusing so much on proprietary technologies and worked together to make sure their products were designed to be compatible; people would buy and use more home electronics.[9] Have you ever tried to install a home-theater system and found it impossible to make the individual components work together, even if they are from the same manufacturer? Kleisterlee argues that the dozens of proprietary technologies currently in existence primarily serve the needs and interests of manufacturers, not customers. In a 2004 interview in CN-NMoney, Kleisterlee said, "The first guiding principle should be that the consumer always comes first. If a product requires a manual, maybe it's too complex."[10] Perhaps if manufacturers cooperated to create common standards, rather than trying to win competitive advantage by promoting their own approaches, everyone would win. The challenge for companies is to find a balance wherein they are able to create complementary relationships with both the customer and other companies while still meeting their own needs.

Companies also need to beware of themselves. Companies can sometimes become so selfish and insular that they only focus on what's good for the company and forget about the customer. This kind of corporate myopia can lead to bland or irrelevant products that simply don't sell. Automobile companies constantly attempt to sustain profitability by sharing components, because it's easier and cheaper for them. There is so much more information on automobiles available now, however, that customers are becoming increasingly aware of an automobile's underlying components. Changing surface cosmetics only is becoming a self-defeating tactic. The buyer of a Toyota may like the idea that it shares many of the same components as a Lexus sedan, for example, but the buyer of more expensive Lexus might not be so charmed.

Customers must experience an automobile's distinctiveness fully enough with all five senses to obtain a sense of its character and "feel" – qualities that go beyond the rumble and hum of the separate mechanical parts. If the feel of a vehicle is distinctive enough, it can even be the core of a brand itself. Consider how the rumble of a Harley-Davidson motorcycle engine has inspired legions of customers to embrace the Harley motorcycle experience. People don't necessarily ride Harley's just to get around; they ride them to make a personal statement and to experience a lifestyle. In many ways, the character and brand are more important than the operation of the motorcycles themselves. Indeed, part of the "Harley experience" is spending a great deal of time maintaining the look and feel customers have purchased.

Customer interactions with products should be viewed from a social rather than a physical or technical perspective, because communicating with the customer is what a product does. Consequently, the relationship between a company, its product, and its customers needs to be built on trust, not unlike a relationship between two people. Often, products with superior technology fail because the designers are unable to see their creation through the eyes of the customer. They mistakenly assume that customers have all kinds of prior knowledge to draw upon and end up designing an interaction that does not make sense. Have you ever tried a product and quickly realized that the designer did not have you in mind when they created it? It happens all the time. On the other hand, have you ever tried a product and found it to be so intuitive that you immediately knew how to use it? That's how it should be.

Quality interaction design fits customers' expectations and how they think. When designs fail, it is often because of poor planning and mistaken assumptions. Design pitfalls to watch out for include:

- **Putting lipstick on a pig:** Cosmetics can't fix poor design. Establishing a superior customer experience through sensitive interaction design requires an understanding of both the psychology of the customer and the communication dynamics of design. For example, Samsung decided to differentiate itself through design rather than hardware. The company invested in design centers around the world and spends a great deal of time studying how customers use products at all the touch points, from packaging to manuals to the actual device itself. In the discovery process, their focus is on determining what interaction is most usable, and what form appeals most to customers. They then build the product and technology around those discoveries.[11]

- **The customer shouldn't have to look under the hood.** Often, companies trap themselves by focusing too much on the technology and not enough on the task the technology is designed to accomplish. As Nicolas Hayek, chairman of the Swatch Group, suggested: "If you can combine powerful technology with the fantasy of a six-year-old, you can create miracles."[12] For years, Apple focused on the cool designs of its computers, but when it finally decided to focus entirely on the tasks its computers were built for, it came up with the Apple iMac G5 (now the standard Intel-based iMac), which is essentially a computer without the computer. It's a flat-panel display on a stand that happens to have a computer inside. All the technology (processor, speakers, disk drive) is hidden in the screen. Apple VP Greg Joswiak explained, "The computer has gone away. This allows you to focus on what you want to do."[13] MediaPointe, a company that makes switching boxes and video recorders, among other things, for corporate audio-visual networks, has the right idea as well. Most of its products only have one button. Push it, and the product will do what it's designed to do. That's all, because there doesn't need to be anything more to it. In essence, the customer interface has been greatly simplified by focusing on the application embedded in the device. Thus, the degree to which technology can enable the user to achieve their goals as well as be emotionally engaged, satisfied, entertained, and dare we say "awed," the more likely adoption will occur.

- **Less can be more.** Companies often feel compelled to continually add functions and features (often called "feature creep"), which clutter the relationship with the customer with too much complexity. Always consider whether a more fulfilling customer experience could be achieved through simplification. Can you motivate your customers to pay a premium for simplicity? Yes -- the iPod shuffle is a clear example of this approach. Apple actually stripped away most of the shuffle's complexity. The device is small and portable and can be worn around the neck, yet it still has enough music storage to satisfy those who buy it.

By analyzing customers' needs in relation to the product/ service environment and the broader socio-cultural context, a company can develop a *complementary innovation* strategy that minimizes barriers to acceptance and adoption by identifying what layer of the product/service pyramid they are on, and to which layers they can realistically move up. In a 2006 *Harvard Business Review* article, Robert Verganti said of a teakettle that Michael Graves designed for the Italian home-furnishing company Alessi: "Michael Graves' teakettle for Alessi showed its greatest originality in broadening people's expectations of what a kettle was and did and, indeed, the nature of the breakfast experience." The teakettle features a tiny bird that chirps when the water is hot. Later in the article, Verganti said: "There is no such thing as an undesigned object—only an object that is well or poorly designed."[14]

Design needs to occur from top-to-bottom on the product/ service pyramid in order to maximize the amount of value products and services deliver to the customer. Building a superior customer experience requires that companies focus on *all* layers of the product/service pyramid, paying particular attention to how the product interacts – i.e., communicates – with the customer. Ergonomics, usability, aesthetics, work-flow, task analysis – these are all elements of product design – but the goal should always be to make life easier for the customer, not the company. However, by identifying what layer(s) of the product/service pyramid can be changed in the design, it is possible for companies to manage their investment while at the same time improving the customer experience.

Manager Key Takeaways

- Manage conversations so that different people with different perspectives are actually talking about the same aspect of the customer experience; some people focus on available infrastructure, software applications, and technology while others are focused on the design of the user interface and direct customer interaction. Make sure they are speaking the same language.

- Leaders can facilitate conversations by encouraging the team to make all aspects of the customer experience concrete, particularly the actual customer interaction. The more abstract the discussion the more likely there will be misalignments because people will naturally fill in the blanks and make it concrete from their own perspective. Remember, people gravitate to the concrete rather than staying in the abstract.

- Design experiences with the goal of aligning all of the levels of the product/service environment with customer needs and the process.

- When assessing current solutions, identify what specific aspects of the customer experience are inadequate or missing. That's where the opportunity lies.

- "Look deep into nature, and then you will understand everything better." (Albert Einstein): As you try to innovate, have you opened your mind to what nature can provide in terms of inspiration? Aristotle said, "In all things of nature there is something of the marvelous."

- Opportunities for innovation require infrastructure that enables the innovation to be successful: Are there infrastructures that are not being fully exploited for the benefit of customers? Look at the continual innovation occurring by using the Internet.

- Are there opportunities that you can identify now that have the potential to be tomorrow's innovations, once necessary infrastructure is available? Develop future scenarios now and identify what infrastructure needs to be available for it to be successful.

- What applications and customer interactions would create value and excitement for customers? Making the connection between customers' and their needs in terms of their relationship with the offering is the ultimate measure of success; if the relationship stinks, it will fail.

- Have you spent time looking for alternative uses for your offering in different situations and with different customers (one-to-many)?

- Have you identified uses for the offering that are superior to currently available solutions (many-to-one)?

- Have you evaluated customer interactions to ensure that the product/service optimizes the relationship and benefits to the customer?

  - Customer interactions should be viewed as social, not physical or technical relationships.

  - Trying to put lipstick on a pig never works because bad interactions will always be bad.

  - The customer shouldn't have to look under the hood and see all the complexity; it should just work the way customer thinks it should.

  - Less can be more: Adding features and functionality at some point just adds complexity. Just give customers what they need, want, and didn't realize they needed, in an elegant manner.

Chapter 8

Putting the Puzzle Pieces Together: What Does the Picture Look Like?

"Example isn't another way to teach, it is the only way to teach."

~*Albert Einstein*

How can you or your company apply the ideas we've been discussing to the challenge of innovation in your field or industry? The answer lies in applying your understanding of human psychology. To tie together the ideas we have discussed throughout the book, let's now look at three examples in terms of the socio-cultural spheres of influence model and the process-oriented relationship model between customer needs and the structure of the offering.

Examples of Complementary Innovation

We selected three examples -- Apple's overall business strategy, General Motors OnStar™, and implantable electrical stimulation devices -- because they illustrate how a complementary approach to innovation addresses the three primary challenges to innovation discussed in Chapter 1. As you may recall, a *complementary innovation* approach strikes the right balance between equilibrium and disequilibrium, change and no change, habit and routine, and revolution and disruption. The challenge is hitting the sweet spot between sustaining and disruptive innovation, whereby benefits are delivered to customers in a way that excites and energizes them, but doesn't turn their world upside down.

The story of Apple's resurgence represents *crossing the chasm* by building momentum and creating a "tipping point" so that widespread adoption occurs. GM OnStar™ illustrates *layering and enriching a mature S-curve* by creating unique added value and experiences that complement the status quo. Finally, emerging implantable electrical stimulation medical devices illustrate *moving from one S-curve to a new S-curve* by creating scaffolding and bridges between the current solution (pharmaceuticals) and the new one (implantable devices). The shift between S-curves is a shift from the current interaction approach to a new interaction approach, which can create significant disruption to customers and companies.

As you consider these examples, notice how contextual factors play a role in the adoption process. In particular, note how a complementary approach to innovation eases the way for acceptance by minimizing the pain of change and disruption for customers as well as for the company delivering the innovation.

Apple's Business Strategy: Create a Product/Service Tipping Point to Leap the Chasm

Apple is one of the most innovative companies in the world today. Yet Apple was headed toward oblivion and irrelevance a decade ago until Steve Jobs' return in 1997. Apple has always been able to attract a **subculture** of faithful customers, many of whom are slightly anti-establishment and more creative than corporate. Their dominant sphere of influence is self-expression, and they enjoy being thought of as edgy and cool; living up to Apple's motto, "Think Different." One major difference between the Apple of today and the Apple of a decade ago is the ever expanding and broad customer base they have been able to attract.

When Steve Jobs returned to Apple he made an important strategic decision by obtaining the support of an unlikely ally—Microsoft. By persuading Microsoft to invest in Apple and support Microsoft Office and Internet Explorer for the Mac, Jobs assured customers and software developers that the Mac would continue to exist and ensured that Microsoft would not stand in its way. Furthermore, to garner support from software developers, Apple made sure that the OSX operating system made it easier for programmers to write applications and for users to connect peripheral devices such as digital cameras and camcorders to the Mac. These actions calmed nervous customers and software/hardware partners who had worried that Apple was not going to be worth paying attention to. In essence, Apple increased the number and quality of **complementary relationships** it had with other industry players, in particular Microsoft and other software developers. They bought time to focus on their strategy by reducing hostile, negative resistance and, more importantly, keeping their very loyal customers engaged.

Apple's resurgence involved a number of converging, **synchronous** factors in society coupled with a number of strategic leaps of faith. At its core, Apple's success is attributable to their focus on what they do well: ingenuity in technical integration, industrial (aesthetics) and software design (usability and elegance), and most importantly, superior customer interaction and experience design. Looking at it in total, their focus has been on the areas that most intimately touch the customer.

Apple focused on the experience for the typical consumer

from initial exposure, purchase, product set-up, product use, troubleshooting, maintenance, and service. They created a comprehensive, superior customer experience at all the critical customer touch points. They created humorous as well as cool commercials featuring Apple OSX versus PC Windows, iPod, and iPhone. The Apple store experience with its simple but cool store design is where customers can try out products with knowledgeable assistance (Genius Bar). The packaging that their products come in, as well as the actual product design, exudes style. Functionally, their product set-up is very simple; basically, their systems work by just plugging it in. Apple has made common activities easy to do for the typical consumer (e.g., music, photos, video, Internet access, and Dashboard, which provides quick access to common Internet sources such as dictionary, weather, stocks, and a lot more without disrupting other activities). On the service side, Apple does a good job of supporting customers when things are not working with knowledgeable "local" help as opposed to outsourced assistance from other countries.

Of course, Apple's comeback cannot be understood without discussing the wildly successful iPod and iTunes digital music phenomena. One of the key trends enabling the growth of digital music is the maturation of the global communications **infrastructure**, which includes the growing acceptance and adoption of personal computers, along with the ever-increasing robustness of the Internet, better file-sharing capabilities, and widespread broadband connections. The iPod itself couldn't exist without concurrent advancements in several areas of technology **infrastructure**, including digital storage, LCD displays, rechargeable batteries, and MP3 software compression that continues to squeeze more computing power into a smaller space.

The bottom line is that this technology **infrastructure** matured to the point where the long-awaited "convergence" of the digital age could occur. The initial group of innovators and early adopters of digital music joined forces with a broad network of computer aficionados to prepare the rest of the culture for innovations Apple would eventually initiate.

Of note is that Apple was not the first to market with a portable MP3 player and in fact nearly missed the emerging digital music opportunity. Remember all the hoopla about techies, geeks, and computer-literate kids sharing (illegally in many cases) downloaded music from online services such as Napster and Kazaa, and burning their own CDs for personal use (**subculture**)? Some people were transferring their music to portable MP3 digital players, but sales of existing MP3 players were flat. As Steve Jobs readily admitted, he was distracted by the possibilities of video editing and nearly missed the opportunity. In 2000, he finally noticed the millions of young people burning CDs of digital music. Jobs said in hindsight, "I felt like a dope."[1]

What did Apple do that enabled the company to cross the chasm when others before and after failed? A critical, not to be underestimated, decision point for Apple was at the very beginning of their innovation journey. Steve Jobs realized that the overall experience was less about technology and music, and more about an emerging way for young people to create a new social experience and social communication networking opportunity (**needs fulfillment**). The "experience" was about communicating personalized messages, expressing emotions, and creating moods that fulfill social belongingness, esteem, and perhaps even self-actualization needs.

A **social-economic sphere of influence context** shift that was taking place during this time was the aggressive anti-piracy efforts that shut down Napster and the attempt at spreading the message that "stealing" music from artists was wrong. What were the barriers to the legal sale of digital music? Before iTunes, the only *legal* options for purchasing digital music were services backed by record companies that imposed complex legal restrictions on its use, and had web sites that were difficult to use. Apple was able to change the game by transforming the experience of digital music in multiple ways and at different levels of process.

In terms of the business, Apple changed the game by removing many of the legal restrictions of use of purchased music, working with the record companies to make a broad range of music available, and changing the business model to lower the prices from an average of $1.49 per song, to 99 cents. In essence, the lower price attracted more users and did not suggest to the user that each song on an album was of equal value.

Beyond price and restrictions on use, the largest hurdle that Apple was able to address was in the **customer experience** in terms of usability and emotional engagement (**customer interface**). Apple was able to take the cumbersome overall **process** of acquiring, playing, managing, organizing, and trading digital music and made it an easy and rewarding experience by creating iTunes and the iPod (**application, customer interface**). Steve Jobs' first inclination when he recognized the digital music phenomenon was to just add a CD burner to the Mac as a standard feature. If Apple had followed this status quo path and reinforced the current process, one could argue that the digital music industry would still be struggling. Just adding a CD burner to a Mac, or just creating the iPod, or doing both of these things without iTunes, would not have transformed the digital music experience. Furthermore, Apple's strategic decision to make the iPod and iTunes **compatible** with the Windows platform extended the potential customer base significantly.

Apple was able to leverage the advantage of file-sharing services, which does not force customers to purchase entire CDs but rather lets them purchase individual songs, so that they can create personalized compilations for themselves and others. Beyond the usability, the Apple experience provides added **customer experience** features such as the shuffle feature that plays songs randomly, celebrity play lists, genres of music, iMixes listener-created compilations, iTunes essentials with various mood compilations, and the ability to visually experience the music with the Cover Flow view of the music library. They also made the MP3 player itself easy to use as well as **aesthetically beautiful**. Once Apple simplified the digital music experience, they were able to open the eyes of key customers to benefits that go beyond the music itself to style, fashion, and personal expression that creates an emotional and social connection with the product and services as well with other people.

Apple's ability to capture the attention, support, and enthusiasm of key customer constituencies in the **culture** that the record labels coveted gave them incredible leverage with record companies, and also influenced the customer culture to see the purchasing of digital music as cool. One executive observed, "Until Apple, it wasn't cool to buy digital music. This is about getting to that pivotal group of people—the people who buy the cool sneakers and wear the right clothes—and showing them that legally downloading music could be cooler than stealing it."[2] Essentially, Apple was able to create **complementary relationships** by persuading the music industry that it was in their best interests to allow Apple access to their music. Clearly, music companies are now not very happy with the power that Apple has, but at the beginning one could argue Apple drove customer acceptance and adoption of legal digital downloads. A lesson to be learned from this is that good cross company relationships don't often last as the true customer value is realized and one company is perceived to have too much power and/or competitive advantage compared to others.

Apple's superior product design exudes simplicity, style, coolness, and different experiences across the different iPod models, while retaining the same underlying infrastructure and a consistent use model for users (iPods regardless of customer interface essentially operate the same from an interaction standpoint whether it has a screen or not). Apple has been able to refresh the iPod product line quickly to take advantage of cost and performance advancements (memory, display, video), and continues to create new products that attract customers (e.g., iPod, iPod mini, iPod shuffle, iPod nano, iPod classic, and iPod touch). There are people who have a regular iPod, a shuffle, and a nano, and find different uses for all of them. The iPod shuffle is a complementary product to the iPod; one is for exercising and the other is for music library storage and general listening. In fact, a recent radio advertising campaign for an iPod giveaway declares, "There is an iPod for every part of your life."

The cool design and ease of use has allowed Apple to attract evangelists from its loyal customer base as well as a diverse set of other groups—teenagers and young adults, urban professionals, celebrities, soccer moms, educators, and top designers—to spread the news and contagion (across **all spheres of socio-cultural influence**). Having an iPod has become chic and has spilled into other parts of the culture. For example, accessories such as a $1,500 Fendi pink cooper purse that holds twelve iPods, or a special iPod control for a BMW steering wheel, boost its social cachet. Nike+ is a personal training and social networking community for runners where iPod's are linked with devices that track and record runner's workout data, provide support to runners with appropriate music play lists and songs, and links runners with the rest of the running community. The creation of an iPod "culture" can be seen everywhere from Wall Street in New York to hip clubs in L.A., where iPod parties are the height of chic. A regular feature of celebrity coverage is now the inclusion of their favorite iPod playlists. The iPod has even led to the radio-station format called JACK FM, in which music is played in long random sets, without DJ interruptions, to mimic the iPod's shuffle feature. Clearly, customers have caught the iPod bug and it has spread with unprecedented speed, accelerating the ongoing revolution known as "digital convergence."

Although other companies developed digital music players before Apple, none of them could cross the chasm the way Apple did. Apple was able do so because of its complementary infrastructure, application, and customer interface strategy, by deftly orchestrating multiple technical and socio-cultural touchpoints to essentially create their own **synchronicity** that led to a social tipping point for digital content.

A reflection of Apple's strategic shift from its computing roots to a broader presence in multiple parts of the customer's life is its decision to change its name from Apple Computer Inc. to Apple Inc. Apple is no longer just selling computer products, software, and peripherals – rather, it's selling a way of life, a digital lifestyle for the twenty-first century for the everyday consumer. Consider the iPhone personal communicator, iPod touch, Apple TV, and, of course, the venerable Mac in its various incarnations such as the iMac, Mac Pro, Mac Mini, MacBook, MacBook Pro, and MacBook Air. Only time will tell what Apple's cultural influence will ultimately be, but it's clear that elegant **customer experience** design and seamless compatibility between its products and services will be key aspects of the company's strategy going forward. Certainly, they are benefiting from cross selling their products because they create a halo effect (e.g., iPod and iPhone driving Mac sales). The "i" before all its product names symbolizes the degree of personalization and level of user interoperability (if I can use one product I can use the others without any problems) to which the company is committed. In describing its iLife application suite, Apple says, "iLife 06 is the easiest way to make the most out of every bit of your digital life." And this, in a nutshell, has become Apple's overall mission.

Apple may be in the midst of another business transformation (**paradigm shift**). The majority of Apple's profits have traditionally come from **products** (iPod) with the **services** providing support for product sales (iTunes). They have been dabbling with different business models with the iPhone (and iPod Touch) whereby revenues are generated through services and applications rather than hardware sales. For example, Apple has been receiving a percentage of the monthly subscription revenue from their exclusive cell phone partners such as AT&T. Some speculated that Apple dropped the price of the iPhone so that they could increase hardware sales because they saw their profits coming from the services.[3] With the recent release of the 3G iPhone, Apple has moved to a traditional cell phone hardware manufacturer model in which they will receive their profits upfront from a wide range of non-exclusive cell phone carriers. However, with the opening of the iPhone Application store, there are analysts that believe Apple will generate meaningful revenue from the sale of iPhone applications.[4]

Other indications that this may be the case is that Apple has begun rolling out the iTunes Wi-Fi Music Store for free at Starbucks, which will drive customer traffic to them (e.g., use of **infrastructure**, **applications**, and **customer interface** and **positioning** it with a prize customer segment) as well as the growing number of web applications that are available for the iPhone and iPod Touch that were developed by Apple or third-party developers that Apple is encouraging (**complementary partnerships** that allow Apple to enhance the customer experience without expending their resources).

General Motors OnStar™: Create New and Unique Customer Value Through Layering and Enrichment

How does an automobile company differentiate itself when the number of brands and models to choose from is huge, and consumers can afford a wider range of vehicles but are also much more selective? The challenge facing any company in a mature market is finding ways to attract customers to its offerings.

GM has tackled this challenge by creating a service, called OnStar that improves the driving experience and extends the company's involvement with customers over the life of the automobile. According to GM, there are more than four million subscribers to OnStar. GM reduces customer resistance to OnStar and increases the likelihood of adoption by providing the customer opportunities to have **direct personal experience** with the service by providing the safety and security benefits for free in the first year after the vehicle is purchased.

Currently, GM reports a retention rate of over sixty percent after the first year of free service. Despite GM's financial struggles and declining market share, its OnStar service delivers unique value to automobile owners as well as to the automaker. Phil Magney, an analyst with Telematics Research Group, states that automakers can't ignore the importance of in-vehicle technology and communication systems because "services such as OnStar provide automakers recurring revenue through subscriptions, enhance the technological value of the car, and serve as an important tool for enhancing the relationship with customers."[5] GM has an advantage over their competitors because they have had the OnStar service available for a while and have created a patent portfolio to protect their investment.

OnStar is an example of *layering and enriching a mature S-curve* by creating unique added value that complements the current infrastructure. OnStar's value has little to do with the automobile itself, and everything to do with enhancing the driving experience by providing what is essentially an electronic safety net and more.

OnStar leverages several broad cultural trends to generate value for customers (**social and economic sphere of influence**). Mass affluence in the United States has enabled many more people to afford a variety of goods and service such as automobiles with added features as well as many more vehicles; as of 2000, twenty percent of families had three or more cars (**cultural sphere of influence** related to individualism and achievement norms). People also spend more and more time in their cars, and their lives are busier and more chaotic than ever. One conclusion from these cultural trends is that the car has become a major "context" for daily life, along with the workplace and home. People eat and drink in their cars, talk on their cell phones, put on makeup, sing, read the paper, and watch movies and satellite television. Given that people are spending more time in their cars, expectations of cars have expanded beyond just a means of basic transportation and has transformed into a kind of rolling living room, safe haven/ retreat, and office.

OnStar fulfills various **customer needs** and clearly fits into the increasingly hectic lives of customers who see their automobile as more than transportation. OnStar services are organized into various categories or packages such as (www.onstar.com):

- **Safe and Sound:** Services such as automatic emergency services notification when the airbag has deployed, roadside assistance when the car breaks down, remote door unlock when keys are accidentally locked in the car, locating the vehicle if stolen, and dealing with insurance claims after an accident. The key basic need that OnStar provides is to keep people connected to help at all times.

- **Vehicle Diagnostics:** Remote diagnostics that check the status of the vehicle and recommend appropriate action to the owner, including scheduling an appointment.

- **Directions and Connections:** Convenience and information services include restaurant suggestions, hotel reservations, driving directions, and alternative transportation if the vehicle breaks down.

- **Hands-Free Calling:** Voice-activated, hands-free calling that does not require a handset or keypad.

- **Turn-by-Turn Navigation:** Personalized directions to your designated destination.

- **Virtual Advisor:** Personalized Internet-based information such as location-based weather, stock quotes, and local weather.

OnStar service is based on an **infrastructure** that includes onboard automotive sensors and diagnostic systems that communicate with cellular communication and global positioning systems combined with a personalized 24-hour call center service. Using this blend of technology and personal, live operators (**infrastructure**), GM is able to deliver a variety of **applications** and customer **interactions**. The **process** of achieving the desired customer outcome has been optimized with a nice blend of technology and human interaction. For example, imagine that you have just been in a serious car accident where the airbags have deployed and there has been an injury. In this situation, the OnStar technology automatically notifies emergency services and provides a person to speak with who can provide reassurance and security while you wait for emergency services. It's hard to imagine a more personal connection between a company and its customer without actually hiring someone to ride in the back seat.

On the other hand, the **customer interface** in the automobile itself is simple yet powerful. The OnStar customer interface considers the context of use by keeping the customer's eyes and attention on the road as much as possible. It consists of a status light and three buttons: one button for placing and receiving calls, one for connecting to an advisor, and one for priority connection to an advisor for emergency situations. The beauty of the system is that this simple user interaction allows the user to connect to a live person for assistance and in many cases allows the user to interact with the system hands-free by just using their voice. Thus, the **customer interface** is a great combination of technology and personal human interactions.

Using this strategy, GM has been able to create a customer experience that is scalable and flexible. By extending the infrastructure (e.g., additional sensors on the automobile as well as communication and GPS technologies), adding additional applications (e.g., collaboration with partners such as MapQuest), and identifying ways in which the human interaction component can be leveraged for additional value, OnStar can deliver additional customer benefits. For example, it's not difficult to envision OnStar providing other **applications** in the future that would reduce the likelihood of accidents by adding more functionality to the automobile, such as sensors that detect when someone might be falling asleep, tracking eye movements to identify when a driver is not looking ahead, and avoidance technology to notify the driver of oncoming cars or perhaps even take control of the vehicle to avoid a collision.

From a positioning standpoint, OnStar has the flexibility to meet the needs of various types of customers for various situations because the **infrastructure, applications,** and **cus-**

tomer interface are essentially in every OnStar equipped car. For example, some customers may want only the convenience functions while others prefer only the safety functions.

OnStar has been around long enough to build a brand image that associates it with GM. OnStar promotes its service through powerful TV and radio commercials in which actual recorded calls from customers are used to demonstrate the benefits of the service and communicate customer experiences. Potential customers hear real people describing their situation while using OnStar and can imagine themselves in that same situation. The advertisements prompt potential customers to think: "What if that happened to me or a family member? Maybe we should have OnStar."

An interesting social phenomenon is that the OnStar brand image has grown to the point where companies in other industries have created a humorous spoof of the service. A Diet Pepsi radio advertisement makes innocent fun of OnStar, describing a fictitious service called the Satellite Emergency Service that helps customers find the nearest location where Diet Pepsi is available. Offerings that are made fun of are engrained deeply enough into the culture for everyone to recognize the humor, which suggests that OnStar has reached a kind of iconic brand status that they can use to their advantage in terms of social awareness and marketing.

OnStar is an example of how companies can benefit by carefully considering why a product or service should exist and what it should do before trying to develop it. Clearly, GM closely studied customers' relationship with their vehicle, and identified several possible pain points in the driving/ownership experience around which a service could be built. Based on this knowledge, GM created an overall customer experience that provides several targeted, necessary, and welcome services, with the flexibility of expanding the services in the future as new customer needs emerge. The service allows GM to have continued contact with the customer in good times and bad. In particular, it puts the company in a position to help people when they are in trouble and at their most vulnerable, which creates positive interactions between the customer and the company, building and solidifying loyalty.

GM needs to consistently create automobiles with superior quality and reliability while delivering on performance, usability of electronic features and, perhaps most important, style and aesthetics across the various market segments. This will require them to respond to current trends such as rising fuel prices, concerns about the environment, economic challenges in the U.S. with the sub-prime mortgage crunch and credit card debt, and people's changing views of small cars as luxury and personalized rather than just an entry level cheap form of transportation (e.g., Mini Cooper). Once that is accomplished, the next step for GM is to look at their entire customer experience (**process**) and create a seamless positive experience that takes the customer from initial exposure through the car buying and servicing experience; not unlike what Apple did when they created iTunes and Apple Stores along with the iPod. If they are able to accomplish this along with the power of OnStar, we believe they can turn things around.

Implantable Devices: Build Bridges and Provide Scaffolding to Cross the Abyss between S-Curves

Mary Shelley's classic novel *Frankenstein* describes how Dr. Frankenstein creates life, assembling parts of dead people and bringing them to life by harnessing the electrical power of lightning. Modern medicine has not come quite that far, but if you consider the use of electricity in pacemakers and defibrillators to keep heart muscles beating, Shelley's ideas were not so far-fetched. As Dr. Stephen N. Oesterle, chief medical officer at Medtronic Inc., said, "The body is on fire with electricity. If you start with that concept, then all you need is imagination."[6]

Implantable devices that use electricity are being used for a variety of health conditions. Such devices mimic, fool, or alter human functioning to provide benefits to the patient (e.g., electrical stimulation to short-circuit pain signals). Besides the established cardiovascular conditions (slow heart rate, fast heart rate, heart failure), the range of conditions where implantable devices show promise include angina, chronic pain, incontinence, deafness, epilepsy, depression, obesity, stroke paralysis, cerebral palsy, head trauma, Parkinson's disease, obsessive-compulsive disorder, bulimia, migraines, and gastroparesis. Implantable devices can direct electrical stimuli to keep the heart beating, or reduce chronic pain in the spine. From our product/service pyramid perspective, then, implantable electrical devices serve as a bridge between two **natural resources** -- the **human body** and **electricity** – and provide an **infrastructure**, namely, a mechanical device that generates and delivers the electricity.

Implantable electrical stimulation devices are an emerging solution that illustrates the *abyss of moving from one S-curve to a new S-curve* whereby the devices are competing with current pharmaceutical solutions.

An overarching trend influencing the society at large and the field of medicine in particular is the dramatic increase in human life expectancy during the twentieth century. In 1901, life expectancy in the United States was 49 years, whereas the most recent data puts life expectancy at 77.6 years and rising. The changes in life expectancy have primarily been due to improvements in public health, medicine, and nutrition. In earlier times, people were more concerned about **basic physiological and safety needs** such as food, shelter, and avoiding premature death from various maladies and infectious diseases. As circumstances have changed, expectations about life have also changed in the developed world. Medicine has made dramatic strides in both the treatment of disease and the management of health in general. The focus has shifted from basic prevention and treatment of major ailments to a focus on optimizing and enhancing quality of life on a day-to-day basis, regardless of age (**shift in needs**).

One consequence of these advances is that people now expect more from their doctors, and from their bodies. People feel they should be able to do whatever they want to do, regardless of their age, and they want modern medicine to assist them in their quest for eternal youth. J. Walker Smith, president of Yankelovich Partners, found in one study that baby boomers defined *old age* as being three years after the average American is dead. "Baby boomers literally think they're going to die before they get old," said Smith. "They fully expect that advances in health care and genomics are going to enable them to live past one hundred."[7] **(Cultural and social and economic spheres of influence)**

Conflicting cultural beliefs revolving around U.S. views of individualism, achievement, freedom, and happiness play out differently in different parts of the population (**cultural**). Within this context, personal freedom and happiness can be defined in terms of personal choice and/or personal responsibility. In general, mass affluence in the U.S. provides people access to a seemingly unlimited choice of options and in many cases people take advantage of it. So many Americans eat too much fast food, don't exercise enough, and generally have a hard time saying no to any enjoyable activity, no matter how counterproductive it might be to their health. According to a recent *New England Journal of Medicine* study, two-thirds of U.S. adults are overweight and one-third of adults are obese.[8]

On the flip side, there are those who take an active role in managing their own healthcare and don't have unquestioned trust of doctors. According to a 2005 Pew Internet and American Life Project Report, eight out of ten Internet users looked for health information online related to specific diseases, treatments/procedures, diet/nutrition, medicines, alternative medicines, and experimental treatments. According to the report, "E-patients are creating a new healthcare environment in which the traditional medical model—ruled by the all-wise doctor who tells patients what is best for them—is being challenged by a new model in which empowered patients can access large amounts of medical information and act as partners with their doctors in making healthcare decisions for themselves and their loved ones."[9]

Regardless of which perspective we take, if *things are broken* or we *don't like something about ourselves,* we assume and expect medical science to provide a quick fix for us. Implantable medical devices have to overcome cultural, social, and economic forces that generate resistance to their acceptance and adoption. Rising healthcare costs in the United States (e.g., healthcare expenditures account for sixteen percent of the U.S. gross domestic product (GDP) translating into approximately two trillion dollars) puts significant pressure on the healthcare system to justify costs whether it is the government, health insurance payers, and individuals.[10] With the aging baby boomer generation living longer, cost pressures will only increase over time.

A second but related barrier to medical advancements is litigation. TrialLawyersInc.com reports that litigation in healthcare has greatly influenced how the healthcare systems perform and operate. For example, medical-malpractice liability alone represents over ten percent of healthcare costs and in 2003 was the equivalent of $3,300 per family of four in the U.S. The report states that liability greatly influences medical practice as well as stifles innovation. In both cases, medical professionals and companies that develop products tend to behave in a status quo manner for fear of being sued.[11]

Patients, healthcare professionals, and the government are scrutinizing the safety and effectiveness of medical device treatment because of recent recalls, litigation, and healthcare costs. With recalls of pharmaceuticals (Vioxx) and medical devices (defibrillators), patient safety has become a top concern. Patients have become sensitized to the potential negative consequences of drugs and devices and are now cautious about their use (**resistance**). There is also greater scrutiny of the short- and long-term safety of medical solutions from a variety of sources such as governmental agencies (FDA, Congress), patient advocacy groups, and patients themselves. In this environment, medical products, including medical devices, require larger and larger clinical trials that last a longer period of time in order to address the risk and uncertainty revolving around safety and litigation for regulators, insurers, and the general public.

Drugs seem to be the answer to all our problems. Overweight? Take a pill. Feeling depressed? Take a pill. Feeling anxious? Take a pill. Arthritis, lower back, body pain? Take a pill. Problem with constipation? Take a pill. A fungus under your toenail? Take a pill. Trouble eating raw vegetables? Take a pill. Over the past decade, the number of prescriptions has increased by two-thirds to 3.5 billion. In 2005, Americans spent as much on drugs as they did on gasoline, the equivalent of $850 for every American. Furthermore, the pharmaceutical industry has flooded the media with advertisements for drugs to treat just about every conceivable condition—to the tune of four billion dollars in 2004.[12] Consumers are now regularly "educated" about syndromes or ailments they didn't even realize they had, then encouraged to rush to their physician and ask for the drug that will treat them.

Pharmaceuticals seem to be the ideal solution for treating most medical conditions because everyone is used to the idea of taking them; it is a relatively easy process to take them, and pills are less mysterious for all of us compared to exotic looking devices. However, many sources, including the American Heart Association (www.americanheart.org), identify and summarize the challenges of taking medications appropriately and in compliance with instructions. The statistics suggest that good intentions, and the ease of use of pharmaceutical solutions (process), don't necessarily translate into compliance, which results in unintended outcomes:

- "The No.1 problem in treating illness today is patients' failure to take prescription medications correctly, regardless of patient age."

- "At any given time, regardless of age group, up to fifty-nine percent of those on five or more medications are taking them improperly."

- "More than half of all Americans with chronic diseases don't follow their physician's medication and lifestyle guidance."

- "Two-thirds of all Americans fail to take any or all of their prescription medicines."

- "Adverse drug reactions (ADRs) may be the fourth-to-sixth leading cause of death. Serious ADRs occur in 6.7 percent of hospitalized patients."

In order for implantable medical devices to become the mainstream solution, key stakeholder groups, namely governmental regulatory agencies, insurers, physicians, and finally patients, must be convinced of its value, so that they are willing to shift from pharmaceuticals to implantable devices for various clinical conditions. A *complementary innovation* approach to innovation recommends that medical device companies use scaffolding to help all stakeholders make the leap to a new way of thinking. Scaffolding, as we have discussed, involves providing people support so that they can make the shift from the familiar to the new.

Throughout the book we have discussed how the design of superior customer experiences requires an understanding of the psychology of innovation so that innovators can surmount the natural human tendency to resist change and preserve the status quo. What can medical device makers do to shift the focus from pharmaceuticals as the solution of choice to medical devices as the solution of choice, or at least as a highly sought after alternative? Implantable device makers have generally focused on therapeutic solutions that are generally closed loop, treating the patient with high precision and immediacy and not requiring the patient's involvement at all. What if device makers changed a few of their assumptions? How would the expanded solution space look then?

Broaden the process of where device makers provide value to people (even before they become patients): If medical device makers shift their focus and broaden their thinking by expanding where and how they deliver clinical benefits, they can play a larger role in keeping people healthy across the entire personal healthcare **process** from preventing to treating conditions.

1. Prevent me from getting sick by helping me avoid issues;

2. Encourage me to stay healthy by keeping me on top of things;

3. Treat my condition; for example, save my life when a life-threatening event occurs.

GM's OnStar is an interesting solution metaphor for medical device makers to think about as they consider extending their value across the personal healthcare process. In essence, what we are proposing is OnStar for the patient, providing safety and security features (treat my condition in life threatening situations automatically not unlike automatically calling emergency services when my airbag deploys and then checking in with me) to preventive services (provide me information about how I am doing regularly and suggest behavior and lifestyle changes not unlike sending me monthly preventative maintenance updates on my car with service recommendations). Perhaps, an interesting way of developing the idea is to use OnStar as a design metaphor whereby a superior patient experience can be created through the combination of an infrastructure (e.g., device, network), applications (e.g., detects and identifies events that person cares about), customer interfaces (e.g., personal assistance, web, phone interactions) to meet patient needs at different phases of their personal healthcare.

Implant and Beyond:

One advantage of an implantable device is that, once implanted in the patient, it is there all the time and can provide the therapeutic and diagnostic benefits with or without the patient's participation. However, an obvious challenge is to get the device in the patient's body with as little invasiveness, discomfort, and inconvenience. An emerging trend that reduces the resistance to device implants for patients is the rise in non-medically necessary cosmetic procedures. According to statistics from the American Society of Plastic Surgeons, 9.2 million cosmetic plastic surgery procedures were performed in 2005, up twenty-four percent since 2000.[13] Consider the popularity of television programs *Extreme Makeover, Dr. 90210*, and *Nip/Tuck* as examples of the expansion of the general population's acceptance of surgery.

Once the device is implanted, the hurdle becomes *living* with the device. Patients expect all the life-saving and quality-of-life benefits while at the same time expecting the device to fit into their lifestyle with little bother or adjustment. Clearly, simplicity and ease of use of (patient interactions with) the device on a daily basis is critical for acceptance and adoption. So, for companies making these devices, it's not only essential that the device work, but that it work within the psychological and physical boundaries patients and family members are willing to accept.

The focus for clinicians is to provide quality patient care, maintain profitability, and avoid litigation. Thus, device makers must focus on creating a clinician experience that optimizes their clinical practice to meet the needs of the patients throughout the process of implanting the device, and effectively and efficiently managing patients on an ongoing basis. Simplicity and ease of use with key functionality for the clinician is required.

Shifting one assumption can open potential opportunities for implantable device makers: What if device makers made the assumption that an implanted device and/or other technology, such as sensors, did not have to be implanted in the body to provide clinical value to people? The requirement for an implanted device is a high degree of precision, immediacy, accuracy, and reliability when it comes to providing lifesaving therapy; however, for other diagnostic and monitoring situations, this requirement is not as stringent and/or necessary. We believe that implantable device makers should explore whether external technologies can deliver "good enough" performance for certain clinical conditions and situations and replace the need for implantable devices. Various external, "wearable" technologies are now capable of providing physiologic, activity-based, and other forms of data applicable to personal healthcare. For example, sensors that track heart rate, respiration, glucose levels, and track activity are now available. Many of these sensors, as well as switches, are getting smaller and smaller to the point that they can be embedded in fabrics. Combined with technologies such as GPS watches, cell phones, iPods, and Bluetooth, many healthcare applications can be created that deliver clinical value without requiring an implant.

Shift from the technical to the social: Helping people live with chronic diseases, and improving the quality of their lives, often requires people to change their behavior and lifestyle choices. Whether the solution is an implantable device or pharmaceuticals, significant hurdles for successful clinical outcomes are compliance and other behavior and lifestyle choices made by patients. Technology can reliably treat the patient when it is required. However, technology (particularly the device) will not solve the issues surrounding patient behavior and lifestyle, which also greatly influence patient outcomes because these require a partnership with technology and people. Perhaps, implantable device makers can create a patient experience that fosters relationships and communication between the patient and their device, the patient and their clinicians, the patient and their family and caregivers, and maybe even between clinicians. Device makers should consider a variety of ways to improve compliance, behavior, and lifestyle changes by rethinking the problem as a social and personal empowerment and engagement issue rather than a technical one that requires a technology solution.

Getting people involved in their own healthcare and encouraging them to live healthy lifestyles requires social support as much as it requires technology solutions. From a social and relational perspective, the healthcare experience should create feelings of intimacy, loyalty, and affiliation that expand patients' social network, increase their desire to fit in, and build positive relationships with its members. These positive social feelings bring an individual closer to others, which can make personal challenges seem less difficult, risky, and scary when done in a group rather than done alone. Providing support and accountability makes behavior and lifestyle change more likely and leads to better health (e.g., someone perceived to be closer to a person is more likely to influence them than a stranger). Examples of social network solutions include Nike+ and PatientsLikeMe.com, which provide social networking opportunities for those on either side of the healthcare continuum: Nike+ is for people who are interested in keeping in shape, tracking their progress and setting personal goals but, just as importantly, connecting with others and competing against them in events such as virtual marathons. With PatientsLikeMe.com, those with specific conditions can become a part of a community for support and information sharing about their condition, symptoms, and potential treatments.

Spheres of Influence

Widespread acceptance and adoption of implantable medical devices will require an approach that addresses resistance across all spheres of influence from the overall culture all the way to the interaction between the product/service and the individual. The key is recognizing the role of psychology in the entire medical device experience, including clinicians and patients, and working to meet the needs and optimize the experience for all involved. Major areas of focus are:

Cultural Sphere of Influence

Many of the trends and customer behaviors described above are specific to the United States. Cultural beliefs, norms, and values affect acceptance and adoption of new solutions. Cultures differ in their attitudes on major issues such as life, death, aging, and the degree to which personal choice is involved. For example, in some countries, assisted suicide is acceptable, while in others it is not. In terms of medical care, Europe evaluates the safety and efficacy of medical solutions, but at some point they leave some degree of personal choice and responsibility for clinicians and patients to determine the best course of action. Perhaps, it is not coincidental that CE mark in Europe comes before FDA approval in the United States.

Social and Economic Sphere of Influence

Understanding the **social** and **economic context sphere of influence** in different geographies is critical, because a one-size-fits-all approach does not work. Issues such as personal responsibility and litigation, technology availability and acceptance, philosophy of medical care and openness to new remedies (e.g., herbs, massage, and acupuncture), cosmetics and appearance – all of these are factors that need to be considered by companies that want to extend the reach of implantable medical devices around the world.

The saying "follow the money" has a significant affect on whether implantable medical devices will become a solution of choice over pharmaceuticals for specific conditions and situations. Resistance to change and the desire to preserve the status quo within the healthcare industry needs to be addressed. The various players have a vested interest in keeping things the way they have always been because they perceive that is the way they continue to be successful.

Some have argued that by partnering with and complementing key network hubs that have a broad range of relationships, the innovator can increase the access and availability of the solution to customers while reducing the network hubs' resistance and outright hostility toward the innovator. This is a win-win situation for the innovator, the network hubs, and the patient. One key network hub relationship that medical device makers need to consider is with pharmaceutical companies. Perhaps by showing how the combination of pharmaceuticals and devices add clinical therapeutic and diagnostic value as well as economic value to pharmaceutical companies, resistance will be reduced. A second network hub to be addressed is between medical device makers, various physician specialties, and hospital systems. At least in the United States, various physician specialties have created organizations and standards of practice that specify who is able to do what procedures. These standards have led to payment systems that reward particular skill levels, care practices, and procedures. For example, if a physician has to "give up his/her patient" to another physician for the device to be implanted, and thus losing revenue, the less likely they will recommend a device, particularly if the clinical outcome is not significantly better than pharmaceuticals, which the physician is able to prescribe. The challenge is to create a complementary situation in which hospitals and various physician specialties remain profitable while still being able to treat their patients more effectively.

Immediate and Individual Sphere of Influence

Earlier we talked about how device makers could expand social networks with web sites such as PatientsLikeMe.com and Nike+. Clearly, the degree to which people are connected to each other as well as to their own healthcare, the greater the likelihood they will change their behavior and lifestyle to enhance their health. Creating advocacy and evangelism for medical devices is critical to acceptance and adoption.

Beyond the social support and viral marketing, device makers need to focus on the core interaction and experience. First and foremost, it has to work. Taking a complementary innovation strategy approach, device makers should consider more carefully what people think about taking pharmaceuticals. Most people, including clinicians and patients, think about medications in terms prescriptions, doses, and drug interactions; device makers should consider this when creating interactions. Creating an experience and interaction that reduces resistance is the goal. Create a feeling of confidence that it works. Consider comfort and convenience so that the experience is not cumbersome, irritating, or bothersome. Ideally, a medical device can be seen as "cool" and aesthetically appealing (e.g., a fashion accessory or badge of honor) so that it turns into a personal statement, and is proudly adorned by the bearer. That increases compliance and turns people into advocates.

Medical device makers have to take into account the spheres of influence as well as simultaneously address the 4P's of innovation in order to be successful. Not unlike Apple, medical device makers need to redefine what they do, who they serve, and how they deliver benefits (e.g., **paradigm**). By broadening their approach they have a better chance of shifting the **paradigm** from pharmaceuticals to devices. They need to play a larger role in the personal healthcare **process** by **positioning** themselves as a provider of solutions that help people be and stay healthy (preventative diagnostics) as well as treat them when they are sick (therapy). Device makers should consider **product** solutions that don't have to be implanted as well as **services** that a broader range of people (**positioning:** healthy people, patients, caregivers, family members) are willing to pay for themselves regardless of insurance coverage (paradigm: business model). Another alternative is for device makers to focus on making their systems **compatible** and easily integrated into the existing hospital **infrastructure** so that **applications** and **customer interfaces,** both clinical and non-clinical [inventory management, billing, documentation], can be created to deliver improved patient outcomes in a more cost effective manner. Making the process of acquiring a medical device easier would greatly improve the customer experience for everyone involved and differentiate the medical device company from its competitors.

As these three case-study examples illustrate, a key part of the innovation process is taking into account the whole socio-cultural context in which the customer lives – their country, culture, educational background, exposure to media, etc. It also means being extraordinarily aware of the subtle cultural and behavioral shifts taking place in society, as well as the possibilities opened up by explorers on the edge of technological innovation. A *complementary innovation* strategy provides a framework for discovering creative new possibilities, and increases the likelihood that the innovation one ends up with is not something that ten other companies are working on at the same time. It also increases the probability of flushing out bad ideas and avoiding wrong turns on the road to successful innovation.

Chapter 9

The Innovation Journey: Taking the next step

"Do not go where the path may lead, go instead where there is no path and leave a trail."

~Ralph Waldo Emerson

"You miss 100% of the shots you never take," and, *"I skate where the puck is going to be, not where it has been."*

~Wayne Gretzky

All companies try to figure out how to reap the benefits of successful innovation; however, innovation also brings with it a certain amount of fear and apprehension about giving up the foundation of the company's current success for the promise of greater success with something less understood. This challenge is reflected in the top three innovation obstacles identified in the 2007 BusinessWeek-Boston Consulting survey: (1) risk adverse culture, (2) slow development times relative to swiftly changing market dynamics and (3) a lack of coordination around innovation activities.[1] Companies have been destroyed by changes made too fast or too slowly; finding the right balance between risk and reward is crucial. The challenge is to maintain equilibrium and stability while also allowing for enough diversity of thought and action to foster rather than stifle innovation. Companies such as 3M are consciously trying to manage their culture to balance between efficiency and innovation.[2]

Our contention is that successful innovation requires a deep appreciation of psychology because innovation is about the underlying psychology of individuals, groups, and cultures. Competitive advantage comes from leveraging an understanding of the common psychological principles that influence people's thinking and actions.

Today's business literature is filled with organizational techniques to break down the psychological barriers that exist in organizations. Some companies take a bottom up while others take a top down approach. Google and 3M encourage employees to pursue pet projects with a portion of their work time.[3] Apple and General Electric drive innovation through leadership vision and mandate.[4,5]

In other cases, companies formally or informally separate the innovation effort from the established culture to shield and protect the employees and the opportunity. Motorola created the Razr cell phone, by creating super-secret teams that worked outside the normal restrictions of the company. Roger Jellicoe, the project manager for Motorola's Razr phone said: "Anytime you've got something radically different, there will be people who feel that we should be putting our resources into other stuff. It was a kind of lock-the-door-and-put-the-key-under-the-mat approach to product development."[6]

Some companies intentionally create relationships among people from different parts of the organization to combat silos and foster information sharing and diversity of thought among functional groups and business units. Johnson & Johnson focuses its efforts on cooperation among its various business units in order to identify and pursue opportunities outside of any current business.[7] BMW coordinates innovation by co-locating cross-functional teams adjacent to their Research and Innovation center.[8] Procter & Gamble's "connect and develop" strategy connects internal groups with a network of external resources that can help P&G identify and develop new products. P&G's strategy is to overcome the dreaded "Not Invented Here" bias that frequently limits organizations.[9]

Clearly, there are many ways to create a successful, innovative company culture that overcomes the built-in organizational immune-system response to change and preservation of the status quo. Regardless of the path that a company takes, its leaders must be aware of and leverage their knowledge of psychology to do it.

Just because an approach worked for one company does not mean it will work in another company, because each company is comprised of different psychological dynamics. Again, there is *no single formula* for innovation, no foolproof set of steps to run through – rather, innovation is an exploratory journey that requires patience and a willingness to adapt behavior so that ideas can be nurtured and turned into real value for customers and companies.

Now it is time to bring the discussion full circle and touch on how leaders can transform the psychology of resistance and status quo preservation into the psychology of innovation and intelligent risk-taking. The following guidelines will help leaders tackle the innovation challenge:

Know thy self before proceeding into uncharted territory

Leaders of innovation need to first honestly assess their organizational culture to determine the best way to influence it to embrace innovation. For example, companies have different organizational personalities that reflect what they do well and how they differentiate themselves from the competition. Is it through hassle-free service at a low price (operational excellence), a superior experience for specific customers (customer intimacy), or through superior product performance (product leadership)?[10] Understanding organizational culture and its *personality* helps leaders determine the best way of forging positive, constructive change.

Swimming upstream against the psychological current

The weight of legacy and the current orthodoxy often paralyzes organizations that recognize they need to change. In times of stress, change, and uncertainty, leaders need to recognize that behavior and decision-making will probably not be driven by rational thought but rather by emotion and instinctual survival behaviors (e.g., protect self and allies and undermine the perceived enemies who advocate change).

We propose a *complementary innovation* approach that recognizes people's tendency to resist change. Leaders need to find ways of stirring the pot just enough to create creative energy, rather than settling for the status quo, while not causing significant disruption.

Herding Cats

Leaders need to be aware of and sensitive to people's inherent cognitive biases and individual personalities and how they affect people's thoughts and actions when it comes to innovation. They need to recognize that groups develop their own explicit and implicit norms, values, and orthodoxies that often lead to a silo perspective (e.g. marketing, development).

Leaders need to play the role of a translator and bridge builder to get the various groups to speak the same language, or at least to appreciate that they are all speaking about the same thing from different perspectives. Effective innovation conversations require a shared set of assumptions and a common vision of what is being pursued. Think about it: If everyone in the room does not share at least some ideas in common about a problem or its solution, and doesn't understand the underlying assumptions that led up to the problem in the first place, how is it possible to consider risks, or make good decisions? Facilitating conversations around the 4P's of innovation (position, process, product/service, and paradigm) is an effective way to make sure that everyone is thinking about the same desired customer experience.[11] Clearly, overcoming people's tendencies to see the world from their own egocentric perspective is a necessary prerequisite for optimized innovation.

Leaders need to motivate and convince the organization that change is necessary. A compelling case needs to be created that captivates and motivates people to action and inspires them to follow the leader's vision by taking facts and figures and bringing the vision to life. In his book *Story: Substance, Structure, Style, and the Principles of Screenwriting,* Robert McKee argues that stories "fulfill a profound human need to grasp the patterns of life—not merely as an intellectual exercise, but within a very personal, emotional experience. In a story you not only weave a lot of information into the telling, but you also arouse your listener's emotions and energy."[12] Grabbing the heart of the organization unites them around a common goal and vision of the future.

Setting the boundaries: Make it less fuzzy and frustrating

Innovation teams are often chartered to be creative and to "think out of the box," with few or no constraints, but at the same time there is great momentum to get things done quickly. This often leads to coming up with ideas that incrementally build on familiar solutions. Leaders need to set a clear set of assumptions and boundaries for innovation activities from the start. A good way of scoping innovation initiatives is provided by Barnes and Conti Associates, Inc. and David Francis in their Managing Innovation workshop (2007). They describe a process in which teams first define their *opportunity space* (what you could do, in other words specifying the river banks) and then focusing on the *innovation agenda* (what you will do in this and subsequent efforts).[14] This provides long- and short-term boundaries and focuses teams and individuals participating in innovation efforts and reduces uncertainty, stress, and resistance.

Intelligent risk-taking: Look at risk in a different way

As we have discussed throughout the book, resistance to change and the desire to preserve the status quo is a challenge all companies face. In many cases, the more successful a company has been, the more difficult it is for them to change because of their success. Success often leads to the endowment effect, which biases people to hang on to what they already have, even if the potential reward is significantly better. Further complicating the situation is the fuzziness and uncertainty surrounding innovation. Uncertainty often leads to too much caution, decision-making paralysis, and an irrational defense of the status quo.

Leaders need to manage the inherent uncertainty and risk associated with innovation by minimizing the fuzziness of the future and the fear of the unknown by taking *intelligent risks*. Intelligent risk-taking involves identifying possible risks whether they are under your control or not, determining whether the potential gain is worth the risk, measuring progress to determine how things are going, and managing through the implementation phase to reduce negative risks and consequences.[14] Thus, leaders must identify, understand, and manipulate the factors that influence the outcome, and monitor the factors that can influence the outcome even if they are not in control of them (e.g., cultural, technology, and other contextual changes).

Given that human psychology tends to encourage resistance to change, the rules for innovation need to be more flexible and adaptive compared to established businesses; plans can change along with circumstances. Leaders need to judge innovation on leading indicators (e.g., customer satisfaction and usability feedback and customer experiences with the developing concepts) as opposed to lagging indicators (e.g., financials) that won't necessarily exist for something that is new and under-developed. Innovation requires leaders to become comfortable with some degree of uncertainty and risk because there will be unknowns.

Pick the right team and provide coaching to improve the odds.

Companies serious about encouraging innovation need to optimize the human resources available in the organization. Leaders need to seek out, identify, recognize, and mentor high potential talent that could be future change agents and visionaries. One prerequisite to success is priming the organizational pump by identifying the required skill sets and behaviors required for the various phases of innovation. For example, when the goal is to search and explore a broad range of options, people need to be willing to let go of the status quo and forget all the reasons why something won't work; who are the people willing to "color outside of the lines?" This might mean getting input from a younger, less experienced employee who isn't jaded by years of wrestling with internal politics.

In every organization, there are people who have unique experiences and backgrounds that, if given the chance, can positively impact a company's decision-making. The people who drive innovation are distinguished by their immense social and interpersonal skills, passion, and ability to entertain other perspectives. They see and evaluate the outside world in unique ways that unearth new opportunities that others don't see. Find the "positive deviants" in your organization who are already doing things differently and bringing their ideas and behaviors into the mainstream organizational culture. Look for people who are, as in the book *The Tipping Point*: (1) the *connectors* who are able to expand and connect beyond boundaries and serve as social glue, (2) the *mavens* who collect and connect pieces of information and then share their knowledge with others, and (3) the *persuaders* who are able to convince others because of their high emotional and cultural intelligence.[15] Also, look for "idea practitioners" who share a set of personality traits outlined in *What's the Big Idea?* by Thomas Davenport and Laurence Prusak: (1) optimism and a belief that people and organizations can change; (2) passion, intellectual restlessness, and devotion to ideas; (3) self-confidence and an ability to get people on board without being self-serving; and (4) boundary spanners who are well connected within and outside of organizations.[16]

Companies that want to be successful need to identify these people, because they are the organization's bench strength – the human resources who will usher in the forces of innovation and transformation. However, every effective team needs a good coach. Leaders need to motivate and rally the team around a vision and strategy and help them navigate the often-treacherous waters of organizational politics. Just as importantly, leaders need to encourage and advocate for the team and protect them from the detractors and hostile forces that often lurk in organizations, particularly ones who have been successful under the old rules of the game.

Designing the experience requires paying attention to the details

The job of the leader is to help the organization recognize the benefits of change in as concrete and tangible a way as possible so that the vision becomes a reality to employees. This is necessary because employees prefer to think about the concrete present, not the abstract future, since thinking about an uncertain, abstract future introduces fear of the unknown.

Leaders also need to be strong advocates for customers and their experience. Given all the angst around change and the associated uncertainties, organizational inertia tends to pull a company's focus and attention toward strategies and actions that optimize for themselves rather than for the customer (e.g., solutions that are easy to implement and/or cheaper to produce). Leaders need to continually focus the organization toward the customer and their experience by encouraging an outward orientation that pushes the organization away from an egocentric, close-minded, insular perspective. Stepping outside in the world provides a fresh perspective. Leaders need to provide opportunities for hunting and gathering new ideas from the outside world. An outward orientation that focuses on unearthing customer insight includes:

- Start with the premise that no market is completely saturated with satisfactory solutions. Search and explore environments, finding gaps where solutions don't yet exist or are inadequate. This approach helps expose opportunities that no one has yet seen.

- Exploring contexts and situations that are outside of the company's core focus provides insight into how other domains are solving similar problems. Perhaps, it is time to leverage other people's work.

- Stepping back and looking at potential megatrends in the cultural context that will influence customers and their experience provides context for the organization's design assumptions.

- Companies often fall into the trap of selectively responding only to the largest and loudest customers. Companies need to be careful not to neglect potential new customers, and to continually step back and evaluate whether those to whom they are paying the most attention are where the biggest opportunities lie. Question and expand what customers the company is pursuing;

truly understand the diverse needs those customers are trying to fulfill, and appreciate the trade-offs customers are willing to make to obtain what they desire.

- Getting a taste of the customer's life by living it for a while is far superior to making assumptions about it based on second-hand or filtered information.

- Understanding all the customer touch points so that the entire customer experience process can be managed is critical. Mapping out the customer experience from top (e.g., value chain: awareness of product/service to actual use to customer service) to bottom (usability of the actual step-by-step interaction between the customer and the product/service) uncovers opportunities for enhancing the customer experience with current offerings as well as potential new options.

- Putting prototype products/services in the hands of customers as soon as possible so that customers can discover its benefits, while at the same time companies learn about the positives and negatives of the customer experience-- a must when it comes to innovation.

Creating the environment takes effort but it's worth it

Leaders need to create an environment where ideas can be nurtured and turned into innovations that deliver value for customers and the company. Richard Ogle, in his book *Smart World*, describes how creativity needs to be looked at from the perspective of the outside world and in terms of interconnected social networks of people, with a recognition that everyone has to set aside their own cognitive biases and filters. He argues that creativity and breakthroughs do not come from the lone genius or hard work but rather from network interactions where ideas bounce around and incubate.[17]

Work conducted at CENTRIM (Center for Research in

Innovation Management at the University of Brighton, UK) focuses on individual and group psychological mindsets and skill sets required for creating an innovation-ready organization that encourages innovation. The research identifies six core organizational capabilities for innovation that organizations need to facilitate innovation.[18,19] They are:

- Leadership that focuses organizational energy around innovation through support and encouragement;

- Talented, competent employees with the right expertise and skills;

- Culture that is infused with implicit and explicit values, norms, and rituals that support innovation such as the celebration of intelligent-risking and "good failures;"

- Learning culture that is always actively pursuing learning about how to deal with risk, how to learn through success and failure, and always listening for diverse views both from within and the outside world;

- Structure and process that is agile, flexible, and adaptive to encourage innovation and guide ideas to completion. The focus is particularly on providing appropriate and systematic structure to encourage creativity while avoiding uncontrolled chaos as well as adapting the process depending on the innovation's maturity;

- Sound decision-making that is strategic and takes into account all relevant internal and external factors (e.g., intelligent risk-taking).

These capabilities are what leaders need to facilitate in their organizational environment. It's about managing the psychology of individuals and the organizational culture that facilitates innovation. Furthermore, managing and leading innovation is about managing oneself and the pressures that are placed on us as leaders. A quote by Lewis Lehro regarding his first years at 3M sums it up well: "Managing and innovation did not always fit comfortably together. That's not surprising. Managers are people who like order. They like forecasts to come out as planned. In fact, managers are often judged on how much order they produce. Innovation, on the other hand, is often a disorderly process. Many times, perhaps most times, innovation does not turn out as planned. As a result, there is tension between managers and innovation."[20] Managers and leaders need to skillfully navigate themselves and their organization through choppy waters that seemingly shift between order and chaos but yet always lead to a clear destination on time.

Conclusion

Innovative companies are successful because they understand how to strategically balance people's tendency to resist change and preserve the status quo (sustaining past and present success) while simultaneously harnessing the tremendous energy released by innovation. Their understanding of psychology provides them a perspective that shapes how they look at themselves as an organization, as well as how they view their employees, customers, and all of the various relationships that bind them together in the marketplace. With this understanding comes the ability to take intelligent, calculated risks, and the emergence of a healthy corporate culture. The corporate culture that emerges balances stability with a productive amount of organizational discontent, desire to push the limits, and to continually improve and change.

With all the talk about what innovative companies, organizations, and leaders possess, ultimately, innovation is about our willingness to act boldly and encourage others to productively challenge the status quo. Patricia Ryan Madson, a drama professor at Stanford University, in describing improvisation sums up the innovation journey well: "…stop trying to come up with something different. Striving for an original idea takes us away from our everyday intelligence, and it can actually block access to the creative process. There is widespread belief that thinking "outside the box" (some call this the goal of creativity) means going after far-out and unusual ideas. A true understanding of this phrase means seeing what is really obvious, but, up until then, unseen...Looking for the obvious offers us a way to approach problems that appear daunting...Do what is natural what is easy, what is apparent to you. Your unique view will be a revelation to someone else."[21]

Are you ready to step up, see the world with new eyes, be willing to appreciate the perspectives of others, and represent the needs of the customer along with the company's needs? Marcel Proust said: "The real voyage of discovery lies not in seeking new landscapes but in having new eyes." Perhaps, most importantly, are you willing to be open, flexible, expect the unexpected, and be prepared to improvise? If you are, then you are ready to begin and lead your own innovation journey that will transform your organization.

Chapter 10

Epilogue: Planning, Preparing, and Presenting the Feast

"Ponder well on this point: the pleasant hours of our life are all connected by a more or less tangible link, with some memory of the table."

~Charles Pierre Monselet

Our goal has been to help you develop the skills necessary to recognize similar nuances and subtleties in the innovation journey so that you can present your customers with superior experiences. As we close this chapter of the innovation journey, we offer a culinary illustration to remind you about the power of a *complementary innovation strategy*. It is about understanding and creating ambience for the customer. As you go on your own journey, keep in mind the power of an innovation mindset that translates into a psychology of innovation rather than a psychology of resistance and the status quo.

Think of innovation in light of a culinary illustration. Our approach to innovation is similar in structure and purpose. The cooking show, *The Iron Chef,* features chefs who are given a key ingredient (e.g., squid, cabbage, carrots) and asked to create culinary dishes that incorporate the ingredient in as many creative ways as they can. The dishes created are influenced by the chefs' backgrounds, tastes, expertise, imagination, and experience. With years of training they are astute at differentiating the nuances and subtleties of flavors, smells, textures, and food presentation and translating it into a superior experience. Will the cuisine be Southern U.S., Asian, European, or Latin American? Will the creation be fried, sautéed, broiled, or served raw? In the hands of these master chefs, ingredients provided by nature—flour, butter, eggs, herbs and spices, fowl, game, seafood, vegetables, and fruits—are creatively modified, and the results are not only varied, but phenomenal! No dish prepared by an Iron Chef is the sort of thing most people would prepare in their own kitchen; they all involve a level of imagination and execution that is beyond the reach of most everyday cooks. Furthermore, the forms in which the dishes are presented go well beyond the functional aspects of taste: the dishes create atmospheres or ambiences of their own. Indeed, presentation is a major part of the experience as well as an important judging category; therefore, every dish is a tiny work of art.

Finally, the judging of the culinary creations is a great example of the niche concept in terms of how their form and function are evaluated. For one judge, the flavor may be too subtle or bland, but the presentation is inspiring. For another judge, a dish may be spectacular for its herbs and spices, but the presentation is flat. Neither judge is right or wrong because they are describing their own experience, but the interaction between the taster and the dish is slightly different in each case. The chef's goal is to score as high as possible in each judging category, but perfection is elusive because of the differing preferences of the judges.

Superior chefs are sensitive to the needs of their customers and truly understand what their customers are seeking. Not only must they use all their skill and experience, they must also put themselves in the shoes of the customer and identify the type of customer they want to appeal to most. If they try to please all of their customers all of the time, they risk being mediocre and uninspiring, with no differentiation. If they are insensitive and egocentric, they risk alienating customers with their arrogant approach (It's hot and spicy or nothing, even if the customer base does not like hot and spicy.). These days, many restaurants have uninspiring, undifferentiated menus that try to meet the needs of all customers in all situations by creating a predictable, uniform experience while attempting to make money through operational effectiveness. The question is whether these establishments are serving the needs of anyone by attempting to serve the needs of everyone.

Many chefs can perform the basics, but award-winning chefs are able to capture the imagination of the customer to deliver delights (unspoken needs) in presentation, taste, and originality. And guess what? They are able to deliver these benefits using the same underlying techniques, processes, and raw materials as their more pedestrian counterparts, but using them in unique and creative ways. Think about chefs who deliver a superior culinary experience by creating fusion dishes that take inspiration from multiple ethnic cuisines and combine them in original ways. It is about being consistently superior while also taking chances so that the superior becomes spectacular. That's innovation! So, are you ready to be the next Iron Chef?

We leave you with some of our favorite inspirational quotes to keep you energized as you begin your own journey toward innovation:

- "Knowledge in depth and in breadth are virtual prerequisites. Unless the mind is thoroughly charged beforehand, the proverbial spark of genius, if it should manifest itself, probably will find nothing to ignite." —Nobel laureate Paul Flory

- "Anyone who has never made a mistake has never tried anything new."—Thomas A. Edison

- "I haven't failed, I've found 10,000 ways that don't work."—Thomas A. Edison

- "The future belongs to those who believe in the beauty of their dreams."—Eleanor Roosevelt

- "It looks impossible till you do it, and then you find it is possible."—Evelyn Underhill

- "Many of life's failures are people who did not realize how close they were to success when they gave up."—Thomas A. Edison

- "If you walk backwards you'll never stub your toe."—Harvey Mackay

- "The finish line is just the beginning of a whole new race."— Susan Saint James

- "Be open to learning new lessons even if they contradict the lessons you learned yesterday."—Ellen Degeneres

- "Read, every day, something no one else is reading. Think, every day, something no one else is thinking. Do, every day, something no one else would be silly enough to do."—Christopher Morley

References

Introduction

1. Tidd, J., Bessant, J., & Pavitt, K. 2001. *Managing innovation: Integrating technological, market, and organizational change.* New York: The Free Press.

2. Kirkpatrick, D. 1998. The second coming of Apple through a magical fusion of man—Steve Jobs—and company, Apple is becoming itself again: The little anticompany that could. *Fortune*, November 9, www.money.cnn.com.

3. Jaruzelski, B., Dehoff, K., & Bordia, R. 2005. Booz Allen Hamilton Resilience Report, Money Isn't Everything, www.strategy-business.com.

4. www.productscan.com

5. Tellis, G.J. & Golder, P. N. 2002. *Will and vision: how latecomers grow to dominate markets.* New York: McGraw-Hill.

6. Zaltman, G. 2003. *How Customers Think: Essential insights into the mind of the market.* Boston: MA: Harvard Business School Press.

7. McGregor, J. 2007. Most innovative companies. *BusinessWeek*, May 14, pp.52-60.

8. Palmisano, S.J. 2003. How the U.S. Can Keep its Innovation Edge. *BusinessWeek*, November 17, www.businessweek.com.

Chapter 1

1. Wilkinson, B., Kopp, D., & Kopp, H. 2003. *The Dream Giver.* Sisters, OR: Multnomah Publishers, Inc.

2. Bowlby, J. 1969. *Attachment and Loss: Volume 1. Attachment.* New York: Basic Books.

3. Mayle, P. 1991. *French Lessons.* New York: Vintage Books.

4. Rogers, E.M. 2003. *Diffusion of Innovations,* 5th Edition. New York: The Free Press.

5. Moore, G.A. 1995. *Inside the Tornado.* New York: HarperBusiness Books.

6. Kim, W.C., & Mauborgne, R. 2005. *Blue Ocean Strategy.* Cambridge, MA: Harvard Business School Press.

7. Chakravorti, B. 2004. The new rules for bringing innovations to market. *Harvard Business Review* 82(3), pp. 59-67.

8. CNNMoney. 2004. Philips: Gadgets too hard to use, January 10. http://money.cnn.com.

9. Carpenter, D. 2005. Motorola reclaims cell-phone design crown. *Minneapolis StarTribune.*

Chapter 2

1. Bronfenbrenner, U. 1979. *The Ecology of Human Develoment.* Cambridge, MA: Harvard University Press.

2. Salter, C. 2008. The faces and voices of Google. February 14. www.FastCompany.com.

3. Kolata, G. 2000. Impotence is given another name, and a drug market grows, April 18, www.nytimes.com.

4. Odell, P. 2007. Fight Club, March 1, www.promomagazine.com/eventmarketing/marketing_fight_club/.

5. Asch, S. E. 1952. *Social Psychology.* New York: Prentice-Hall.

6. Henslin. J. M. 2004. *Essentials of sociology: A down-to-earth approach*, 5ᵗʰ Edition., MA: Pearson and Allyn and Bacon.

7. Flores, F., Letelier, M.F., & Spinosa, C. 2003. Developing productive customers in emerging markets 2003. *California Management Review*, vol. 45, no. 4, pp. 77-103.

8. Piaget, J. 1970. Piaget's theory. In *Carmichael's Manual of Child Psychology*, P.H. Mussen ed. New York: Wiley.

9. Kagan, J. 1984. *The Nature of the Child*. New York: Basic Books.

10. Thomas, A., & Chess, S. 1982. *Temperament and Development*. New York: Brunner/Mazel.

11. Gardner, H. 1999. *Intelligence Reframed*. New York: Basic Books.

12. Gardner, H. 2004. *Changing Minds: The Art and Science of Changing Our Own and Other People's Minds.* Cambridge, MA: Harvard Business School Press.

13. Rogers, E.M. 1962. *Diffusion of Innovations,* 1ˢᵗ Edition. New York: The Free Press.

14. Reber, A.S., & Reber, E. 2001. *The Penguin Dictionary of Psychology,* 3ʳᵈ Edition., New York: Penguin Books.

15. Piaget, J. 1970. Piaget's theory. In *Carmichael's Manual of Child Psychology*, P.H. Mussen ed. New York: Wiley.

16. Capon, N., & Kuhn, D. 1979. Logical reasoning in the supermarket: Adult females' use of a proportional reasoning strategy in an everyday context. *Developmental Psychology*, 15, pp. 450-452.

17. Maslow, A. 1954. *Motivation and Personality,* 2ⁿᵈ Edition. New York: Harper & Row.

18. Coy, P. 2005. Why logic often takes a backseat. *Business Week,* March 28, www.businessweek.com.

19. Gibson, J.J. 1986. *The Ecological Approach to Perception.* Hillsdale, NJ: Earlbaum.

20. Maslow, A. 1954. *Motivation and Personality,* 2nd Edition. New York: Harper & Row.

21. Maslow, A. 1971. *The farther reaches of human nature.* New York: The Viking Press.

Chapter 3

1. Piaget, J. 1970. Piaget's theory. In *Carmichael's Manual of Child Psychology,* P.H. Mussen ed. New York: Wiley.

2. Delta Airlines. 2004. Going global. *Sky Magazine,* November.

3. Christensen, C.M. 1997. *The Innovator's Dilemma.* Cambridge, MA: Harvard Business School Press.

4. Christensen, C.M., & Raynor, M.E. 2003. *The Innovator's Solution.* Cambridge, MA: Harvard Business School Press.

5. Francis, D. & Bessant, J. 2005. Exploring the "Targeting" of Innovation Capability. *Technovation,* vol. 25 (3), pp.171-184.

6. Sutton, R.I. 2002. *Weird Ideas That Work: 11 ½ Practices for Promoting, Managing, and Sustaining Innovation.* New York: The Free Press.

7. Hamm, S. 2005. Beyond Blue. *BusinessWeek,* April 18, www.businessweek.com.

8. Lafley, A.G. & Charan, R. 2008. *The Game-Changer: How you can drive revenue and profit growth with innovation.* New York: Crown Business.

9. Hindo, B. 2007. At 3M, a struggle between efficiency and creativity. *BusinessWeek: Inside Innovation,* June 11, pp 8-16.

10. O'Reilly, C.A. & Tushman, M.L. 2002. *Winning through innovation: A practical guide to leading organizational change and renewal.* Cambridge, MA: Harvard Business School Press.

11. Parade. 2008. A new way to save on gas. *Parade Magazine,* April 6, pp.11.

12. Zachary, P. G. 2007. The unsung heroes who move products forward. September 30, www.nytimes.com.

13. Seybold, P.B. 2001. Get Inside the Lives of Your Customers. *Harvard Business Review, 68(5),* May, pp. 80–91.

14. Hammer, M. 2004. Deep change: How operational innovation can transform your company. *Harvard Business Review,* 82(4), pp. 85-93.

15. Meredith, R. 2005. A tale of two strategies. October 3, www.forbes.com.

16. Schwartz, P. 2003. *Inevitable Surprises: Thinking Ahead in a Time of Turbulence.* New York: Gotham Books.

17. Christensen, C.M. 1997. *The Innovator's Dilemma.* Cambridge, MA: Harvard Business School Press.

18. Seeking Alpha 2006. Apple Stores now more profitable than Tiffany's per square foot, December 26, www.seekingalpha.com.

Chapter 4

1. www.neilsenmedia.com

2. Bianco, A 2004. The vanishing mass market. *Business Week,* July 12, www.businessweek.com.

3. Gibson, E.J., & Pick, A.D. 2000. *An Ecological Approach to Perceptual Learning and Development.* New York: Oxford University Press.

4. Zyman, S. 2000. *The End of Marketing as We Know It.* New York: HarperBusiness Books.

5. Gibson, J.J. 1986. *The Ecological Approach to Perception.* Hillsdale, NJ: Earlbaum.

6. Gibson, E.J., & Pick, A.D. 2000. *An Ecological Approach to Perceptual Learning and Development.* New York: Oxford University Press.

7. Pinker, S. 2002. *The Blank Slate: The Modern Denial of Human Nature.* New York: Penguin Group.

8. Lafley, A.G. & Charan, R. 2008. *The Game-Changer: How you can drive revenue and profit growth with innovation.* New York: Crown Business.

9. Von Hippel, E., Thomke, S., & Sonnack, M. 1999. Creating breakthroughs at 3M. *Harvard Business Review,* 77(5), pp. 47-57.

10. Thomke, S.H. 2003. E*xperimentation Matters: Unlocking the Potential of New Technologies for Innovation.* Boston: Harvard Business School Publishing.

11. Hamel, G. 2002. *Leading the Revolution.* New York: Plume.

12. Gibson, J.J. 1986. *The Ecological Approach to Perception.* Hillsdale, NJ: Earlbaum.

13. CNNMoney. 2004. Philips: Gadgets too hard to use, January 10, www.money.cnn.com.

14. Reinhardt, A. 1998. Steve Jobs: There's sanity returning. *BusinessWeek,* May 25, www.businessweek.com.

15. Lafley, A.G. & Charan, R. 2008. *The Game-Changer: How you can drive revenue and profit growth with innovation.* New York: Crown Business.

16. Kawasaki, G., & Moreno, M. 2000. *Rules for Revolutionaries: The Capitalist Manifesto for Creating and Marketing New Products and Services.* New York: HarperBusiness Books.

17. Heinrichs, J. 2007. Big Fat: A Big Fat Idea. *Southwest Airlines Spirit Magazine*, June.

18. Vygotsky, L.S. 1978. *Mind and society: The development of higher mental processes.* Cambridge: MA: Harvard University Press.

19. Demerjian, D. 2008. Hustle & Flow. *Fast Company*, March, pp. 60-62.

Chapter 5

1. Koffka, K. 1935. *Principles of Gestalt Psychology.* London: Lund Humphries.

2. Bronfenbrenner, U. 1979. *The Ecology of Human Development.* Cambridge, MA: Harvard University Press.

3. www.bugaboo.com

4. Gladwell, M. 2002. *The Tipping Point: How Little Things Can Make a Big Difference.* Boston: Little, Brown.

5. Verganti, R. 2006. Innovating through design. *Harvard Business Review,* 84(12), pp. 114-122.

6. Ogle, R. 2007. *Smart World: Breakthrough creativity and the new science of ideas.* Cambridge, MA: Harvard University Press.

7. Schwartz, P. 1996. *The Art of the Long View: Planning for the Future in an Uncertain World.* New York: Currency Paperback.

8. Bishop, P. & Hines, A. 2006. *Thinking about the Future, Guidelines for Strategic Foresight.* Washington, DC: Perfect Paperback.

Chapter 6

1. Bandler, M. J. 2007. Inside Scoop. *NWA WorldTraveler.* October.

2. Gibson, J.J. 1986. *The Ecological Approach to Perception*. Hillsdale, NJ: Earlbaum.

3. Maslow, A. 1954. *Motivation and Personality,* 2nd Edition. New York: Harper & Row.

4. Maslow, A. 1971. *The farther reaches of human nature*. New York: The Viking Press.

5. Gill, M. G. 2007. *How Starbucks Saved My Life: A son of privilege learns to live like everyone else.* New York: Gotham Books.

6. Silverstein, M.J., & Fiske, N. 2003. *Trading Up: The New American Luxury.* New York: Portfolio Publishing.

7. Palmeri, C., with Kiley, D. 2005. In hot pursuit of Yoga Mama. *BusinessWeek,* November 7, pp. 178-130.

8. Kim, W.C., & Mauborgne, R. 2005. *Blue Ocean Strategy.* Cambridge, MA: Harvard Business School Press.

9. Christensen, C.M., & Raynor, M.E. 2003. *The Innovator's Solution.* Cambridge, MA: Harvard Business School Press.

10. Barret, V. 2008. Here come the Featuretisements. *Forbes*, July 21, pp.50.

Chapter 7

1. Gibson, J.J. 1986. *The Ecological Approach to Perception*. Hillsdale, NJ: Earlbaum.

2. Gibson, E.J., & Pick, A.D. 2000. *An Ecological Approach to Perceptual Learning and Development*. New York: Oxford University Press.

3. www.3m.com

4. Schlender, B. 2005. How big can Apple get? *Fortune,* February
    21, http://money.cnn.com/magazines/fortune/fortune_
    archive/2005/02/21/8251769/index.htm.

5. Park, A. 2004. . For every gizmo, a TI chip. *BusinessWeek,*
    August 16, pp.52-53.

6. www.intel.com.

7. www.cisco.com.

8. Schlender, B. 2005. How big can Apple get? *Fortune,* February
    21, http://money.cnn.com/magazines/fortune/fortune_
    archive/2005/02/21/8251769/index.htm.

9. CNNMoney. 2004. Philips: Gadgets too hard to use, January 10,
    www.money.cnn.com.

10. CNNMoney. 2004. Philips: Gadgets too hard to use, January 10,
    www.money.cnn.com.

11. Rocks, D., & Ihlwan, M. 2004. Samsung design. *Business
    Week,* December 5, www.businessweek.com.

12. www.swatchgroup.com.

13. Stone, B. 2004. Getting iMac right. *Newsweek,* September 13,
    www.newsweek.com.

14. Verganti, R. 2006. Innovating through design. *Harvard Business
    Review,* 84(12), pp. 114-122.

Chapter 8

1. Schlender, B. 2005. How big can Apple get? *Fortune,* February
    21, http://money.cnn.com/magazines/fortune/fortune_
    archive/2005/02/21/8251769/index.htm.

2. Black, J. 2003. Where "Think different" is taking Apple.
    BusinessWeek Online, August 5, www.businessweek.com.

3. Elmer-DeWitt, P. 2007. Apple and AT&T: Who's exploiting whom? October 24, www.money.cnn.com.

4. Elmer-DeWitt, P. 2008. Will the App Store be a cash cow for Apple? [Update].Apple 2.0, June 10, http://apple20.blogs. fortune.cnn.com/category/app-store/.

5. Karoub, J. 2007. OnStar, MapQuest unite in joint venture. April 25, www.money.cnn.com.

6. Arndt, M. 2005. Rewiring the body. *BusinessWeek,* March 7, pp. 74-82.

7. Wingert, P., Springen, K., Reno, J., Samuels, A., Raymond, J., & Adams, W.L. 2005. Hitting 60. *Newsweek,* November 14, pp. 50-58.

8. www.cdc.gov.

9. Fallows, D. 2005. How women and men use the Internet, December 28, www.pewinternet.org.

10. Borger, C., Smith, S., Truffer, C., Keehan, S., Sisko, A., Poisal, J. & Clemens, M.K. 2006. Health Spending Projections Through 2015: Changes On The Horizon, Health Affairs, 25, no. 2, pp. 61-73. www.content.healthaffairs.org/cgi/content/abstract/ hlthaff.25.w61.

11. Trial Lawyers Inc. Health Care: The lawsuit industry's effect on American Health, 2005. www.triallawyersinc.com/healthcare.

12. www.cbsnews.com.

13. www.plasticsurgery.org.

Chapter 9

1. McGregor, J. 2007. Most innovative companies. *BusinessWeek,* May 14, pp.52-60.

2. Hindo, B. 2007. At 3M, a struggle between efficiency and creativity. *BusinessWeek: Inside Innovation*, June 11, pp. 8-16.

3. What's it like to work in engineering, operations, & IT? www. google.com.

4. McGregor, J. 2006. The world's most innovative companies. *BusinessWeek*, April 24, pp.62-74.

5. Brady, D. 2005. The Immelt revolution. *BusinessWeek,* March 28, pp.64-73.

6. Lashinsky, A. 2006. RAZR's edge: How a team of engineers and designers defied Motorola's own rules to create the cell phone that revived their company. http://money.cnn. com/2006/05/31/magazines/fortune/razr_greatteams_fortune/ index.htm

7. Barrett, A. 2006. J&J: Reinventing How It Invents. *BusinessWeek Online*, April 17.

8. McGregor, J. 2006. *The world's most innovative companies.* *BusinessWeek,* April 24, pp.62-74.

9. Huston, L. & Sakkab, N. 2006. Connect and Develop: Inside Procter & Gamble's New Model for Innovation. *Harvard Business Review*, 84(3), pp. 58-66.

10. Treacy, M., & Wiersema, F. 1997. *The Discipline of Market Leaders.* Reading, MA: Addison-Wesley.

11. Francis, D. 2005. A Reference Model Of Innovation Capability And Implications, For Organisational Development, CINet Conference Papers, Brighton, September 2005.

12. McKee, R. 1997. *Story: Substance, Structure, Style, and the Principles of Screenwriting.* New York: HarperCollins.

13. Barnes and Conti Associates, Inc. and Francis, D. 2007. Managing Innovation: Optimizing the power of new ideas. www. barnesconti.com.

14. Barnes and Conti Associates, Inc. 2007. Intelligent risk-taking: From vision to Action. www.barnesconti.com.

15. Gladwell, M. 2002. *The Tipping Point: How Little Things Can Make a Big Difference.* Boston: Little, Brown.

16. Davenport, T.H. & Prusak, L. 2003. *What's the Big Idea: Creating and capitalizing on the best management thinking.* Cambridge, MA: Harvard Business School Press.

17. Ogle, R. 2007. *Smart World: Breakthrough creativity and the new science of ideas.* Cambridge, MA: Harvard University Press.

18. Barnes and Conti Associates, Inc. and Francis, D. 2007. *Managing Innovation: Optimizing the power of new ideas.* www. barnesconti.com.

19. Francis, D. 2005. *A Reference Model of Innovation Capability and Implications for Organisational Development*, CINet Conference Papers, Brighton, UK, September 2005.

20. www.innovationtools.com/Quotes/Quotes.asp

21. Madson, P.R. 2005. *Improv Wisdom: Don't prepare, just show up.* New York: NY: Bell Tower.

Index

A
adoption cycle, 5–10
aesthetic needs, 92, 125, 128
"affordances," 106
"ambidextrous organization," 35
applications, 110–111, 114–115, 132, 134, 135, 149
Aristotle, 121
Aurelius, Marcus, 58

B
Bacon, Francis, 12
"baloney generator," 56
Barenburg, Max, 74
Barnes and Conti Associates, 156
Belasco, James, 1
belongingness, 92
Bessant, John, 32
biomimicry, 109
"The Blind Men and the Elephant," 32
boundary setting, 155–156
Bowlby, John, 3–4
Brinkley, David, 16–17
Bronfenbrenner, Urie, 15, 70–73, 75

C
CENTRIM (Center for Research in Innovation Management), 160–161
change
    resistance to, 2–4, 140, 154
    timing of, 5–6
Christensen, Clayton, 31, 38, 96, 97
cognitive needs, 92
communications infrastructure, 126

About the Authors

Nelson Soken, Ph.D.

Nelson Soken, Ph.D., is systems strategist, senior engineering manager at Medtronic, a medical device manufacturer in Minneapolis, Minnesota. He received his undergraduate degree in psychology from Macalester College and his doctorate in experimental child psychology from the University of Minnesota. He has published in academic psychology journals, presented papers at various professional technology conferences, conducted training workshops on design and innovation topics, and has been an invited speaker on the topic of innovation. Dr. Soken has also taught psychology courses at the university level and has conducted internal corporate workshops in the U.S. and Europe on product planning and human factors topics. Throughout his career, he has been involved in a variety of activities, such as new opportunity identification, product planning, human factors strategy and management, innovation initiatives, knowledge management, competitive intelligence, and leadership development efforts. Prior to joining Medtronic, he was manager of information resources at Honeywell International as well as serving in various senior technical positions both in Europe and the U.S. where he participated in corporate strategy initiatives along with executing on technical human factors activities.

Wil Wengert

 Wil Wengert is the president of a consulting firm, C4 Planning, Inc. He has successfully assisted numerous Fortune 500 companies in identifying new business opportunities. Wil has completed product planning, product development and strategic market research projects in Australia, Europe, the Far East, and the U.S. since 1993. His experience and studies in the area of next generation strategic product planning and disruptive innovation led to the definition of the complementary innovation strategy. He has interfaced with numerous Fortune 500 companies such as Agilent Technologies, American Express, DuPont, Hewlett-Packard Johnson & Johnson, Medtronic, Motorola, United Technologies, and Volvo. Wil has experience working in a variety of industries such as medical, aerospace, transportation, telecommunications, electronics, and utilities. Prior to becoming a consultant, Wil graduated from the business school at the University of Colorado and has worked for United States Surgical Corporation, American Hospital Supply, and Baxter in sales, marketing, and product development.